TEN WORSHIPPING CHURCHES

TEN WORSHIPPING CHURCHES

Edited by
Graham Kendrick

MARC Europe
British Church Growth Association

British Library Cataloguing in Publication Data

Ten worshipping churches.
  1. Public worship
  I. Kendrick, Graham
  264   BV10.2

  ISBN 0–947697–31–4

Unless otherwise noted, Scripture quotations in this publication are from the Holy Bible, New International Version, Copyright © 1973, 1978, 1984, International Bible Society. Published by Hodder and Stoughton. Used by permission.

MARC Europe is an integral part of World Vision, an international Christian humanitarian organisation. MARC's object is to assist Christian leaders with factual information surveys, management skills, strategic planning and other tools for evangelism. MARC Europe also publishes and distributes related books on matters of mission, church growth, management, spiritual maturity and other topics.

The British Church Growth Association is a coordinating body for those interested in the growth (spiritual, numerical, organic and incarnational) of the British Church today. It comprises researchers, teachers, consultants and practitioners who share information, insights, experience, and new thinking through regional and national activities, a regular journal, occasional publications and other resources, seminars and conferences. The postal address is: PO Box 71, London SE11 4PX.

Cover photo by Chris Gander, courtesy of *Today* magazine. Used by permission.

Printed and bound in Great Britain by
Anchor Brendon Ltd, Tiptree, Essex

CONTENTS

TEN WORSHIPPING CHURCHES

1 The Abbey Church of the
  Holy Cross and St Lawrence,
  Waltham Abbey, Essex

2 Glenwood Church, Cardiff,
  South Wales

3 Newhills Parish Church,
  Bucksburn, Aberdeen

4 Ansdell Baptish Church,
  Lytham St Annes, Lancs

5 New Life Christian Fellowship,
  Lincoln

6 Chapel St Methodist Church,
  Penzance, Cornwall

7 Poplars Christian Fellowship,
  Worksop, Notts

8 St Mary's Parish of Ballybeen,
  Dundonald, Belfast

9 Clarendon Church,
  Brighton and Hové, Sussex

10 St Michael-le-Belfrey,
   York

INTRODUCTION

Graham Kendrick

Graham Kendrick, son of a Baptist pastor, grew up in Essex and Southwest London. He trained first at Avery Hill College of Education in Eltham to be a teacher, but then entered into full-time music ministry. His singing and evangelism have taken him as far afield as the United States, Australia and India.

After two and a half years in evangelistic team ministry and a further three years as Music Director for British Youth for Christ, Graham went on to work as one half of the Kendrick and Stevenson music and mime duo. During this time, his involvement in praise and worship steadily grew to become his main work, and today he is best known as the writer of contemporary choruses and hymns.

Graham and his wife Jill and their three daughters lived for five years in York, where they worshipped at St Michael-le-Belfrey—one of the churches featured in this book. Currently the Kendricks live in Forest Hill, just outside London. Graham is now part of the ministry team of the Ichthus Christian Fellowship. In addition to his writing and recording activities, he travels all over the country and abroad leading worship conferences and celebrations and giving seminars for worship leaders, musicians and church leaders. His wide-ranging experience and deep concern for worship that glorifies God come through clearly and joyfully in this introduction.

When the Samaritan woman at Jacob's well posed a question about worship to the Jewish stranger, the apparent simplicity of her words belied the multitude of divisive issues lurking behind them. Not only were there controversies concerning such things as holy places, traditions, priestly lineage and ceremonial procedures, but there were also centuries of religious and racial prejudice.

Jesus, without so much as a pause to comment on these external issues, spoke directly to the heart of the matter, which, if you will excuse the play on words, turned out to be supremely a matter of the heart! The religious people were seeking, with much striving and argument, to determine who had the best location, tradition and liturgy, and who could claim the purest historical roots or the most impeccable doctrine; but Jesus announced what the *Father* was seeking. In the midst of our contemporary debates about forms, styles, traditions and differing interpretations of scriptural commands about worship, often the last question to be considered is what God might be looking for. Jesus declared: 'Believe me, woman, a time is coming when you will worship the Father neither on this mountain nor in Jerusalem … A time is coming and has now come when the true worshippers will worship the Father in spirit and truth, for they are the kind of worshippers the Father seeks. God is spirit, and his worshippers must worship in spirit and in truth' (John 4:21–24). The measure of the true worshipper that the Father seeks is not the length of his historical tradition or the height of his hands above his head, but the depths of the love in his heart for the Father. It has more to do with dimension—'in spirit'—than location, more to do with integrity—'in truth'—than pedigree.

In this book are ten samples of churches who have set as their primary goal that of giving the Father what he is looking for. All would humbly claim still to be wearing their 'L' plates, and none to have achieved all that lofty aim implies. None would claim to have made the progress they have made without cost, struggle and mistakes, but in every case the 'growing pains' are regarded as having been worth enduring for the sake of the fresh release of worship that has resulted. To some minds the developments described will seem daring and adventurous, to others familiar and unremarkable. Yet across the nation we find churches at every conceivable stage of development, and we have attempted to reflect this also. Indeed it is worth pondering upon the likelihood that those who seem furthest on will sooner or later find themselves having gone 'full-circle', returning afresh to basic principles, to re-learn at a deeper level, or to start again with a new generation of people in the congregation.

Although all of the churches featured here have produced excellent results, this book is by no means an attempt to feature the 'ten best' worshipping churches. Such an attempt would be foolish in the extreme, as only the Lord himself could make such a judgement. What is more to the point is that so widespread is the phenomenon of churches pursuing renewal in worship that researching all the possible candidates would take far too long. The samples have been chosen for their accessibility as models and examples from which the 'average' church can learn and gain encouragement, rather than for their ability to score high on an achievement basis. There are no doubt churches that can boast of bigger or better, but we have tried to be representative of the vast and widespread revolution in worship that is a current feature of the church today. So we are not dealing with a few outstanding exceptions against a general background of mediocrity, but with a few pertinent examples within a whole climate of change.

The Holy Spirit seems to be no respecter of denominations, and hence we find similar changes happening across a vast range of churchmanship. From a Methodist chapel in Cornwall describing itself as a 'bastion of tradition and respectability', having historical connections with the mother of the Brontë sisters and with John Wesley himself, to a church of only eight years' vintage in a residential area near Brighton, where free-flowing praise and worship make room for such things as dance, drama, healing and deliverance, and for literal performances of psalms involving clapping, shouting, silence, kneeling, antiphonal chants, musical 'selahs', lying prostrate ... to the accompaniment of choir and orchestra. From the rural surrounds of Aberdeen and a Presbyterian Church of Scotland congregation, where until relatively recently tradition permitted only metrical psalms pitched by a tuning fork, to a recently planted fellowship of Brethren extraction, meeting in a sports hall on a housing estate on the outskirts of Cardiff, where an inspiring story of unity in the midst of diversity unfolded. In addition there are backgrounds, connections and present affiliations with Churches of England and Ireland, Baptist, Assemblies of God, Restoration and Independent 'house fellowships'. To be able to report new life and vitality in worship across such a spectrum, with the bonus that all ten report numerical growth as well, is surely of great significance to the church in this nation, and gives more hope for the future than has been evident for many decades.

How Has All This Come About?

There are doubtless many factors which have brought about this climate of change. The rapid social and technological revolutions of this century have forced the church to accept more rapid change than it would possibly have countenanced a century ago. An age of doubt and materialism, a fading empire and the spirit-crushing horrors of two world wars have combined with other factors to empty the churches of Britain at a colossal rate. A positive result of these negatives, however, has been a drastic decrease in nominal Christianity. Since 1970, church *membership* has declined by 18%; still, *attendance* at church holds at 11%.

Within this remnant, the renewal and charismatic movements have created a groundswell of desire for a more dynamic, New Testament style of Christianity. Numbers in new churches, for example, have grown threefold. Traditional ways have been challenged; there has been a cry for full lay participation, for more freedom of expression for the 'ordinary' worshipper. Individualistic worship has been challenged, and spiritual reality—where God is known, and his presence and power manifested—is seen more and more as a 'norm' to be experienced by the whole body of believers. The rise in popularity of the 'big Bible weeks' has had ramifications that are easy to underestimate. Even in churches where the majority of members have seen no great need to pursue radical change in worship, the newly raised expectations of those who attend these conferences have often forced the issue of worship into view.

Over this freshly ploughed land have blown the seeds of new songs, hymns and choruses, which have criss-crossed the old denominational barriers on an unprecedented scale and with remarkable speed, launched at the above mentioned Bible weeks and conferences, and aided and abetted by new technology of recorded cassettes and other contemporary means of communication. Overhead projectors and screens have sprouted at the front of thousands of churches, providing 'instant' words for the congregation to learn from, and new problems of copyright to wrestle with! The popularity of the guitar has encouraged the playing and writing of simple worship songs to become mass phenomena; and coupled with the advent of the home group fellowship, the performance of worship has been plucked out of the rarified atmosphere of a church building and the exclusive control of ministers, choirmasters and organists, and has been made accessible technically and idiomatically to the ordinary believer. Of course, the ideal of culturally accessible forms of worship is nothing new; for, as the minister of Newhills Presbyterian Church of Scotland points out, Calvin himself believed that the expression of an authentic relationship between God and man must be experienced in the indigenous language and cultural form of the worshipper. How easily the contemporary idiom of one generation, born out of a desire for relevance and clear communication, becomes the obscure and antiquated, yet jealously preserved, tradition of subsequent ones!

The climate of change has made room for much more than new music. Dance, movement, drama, banners and flags, mime, children's orchestras, adults' orchestras, worship bands and public praise processions have been added to the traditional hymns, choirs, solos and organs. Naturally, not everyone will agree that this has been entirely a good thing, and indeed, a lot of dross has been found mixed with the gold. The lowering of musical standards, repetitive singing of songs which lack musical, lyrical or theological integrity (or all three at once!), the leadership of worship passing into the hands of the unqualified, inexperienced or insensitive, objections to the very use of drama, movement or dance at all: these are just a few of the criticisms levelled at the 'new wave' of worship. Many such criticisms do, of course, have validity, yet any new movement is bound to give rise to mediocre and bad practices as well as good ones. There is, however, a growing maturity evident in many, many churches, not least among those featured here, who are now by no means novices in these things. Some, like St Michael-le-Belfrey, York, are able to claim twenty or more years' experience in 'renewed' worship, not to mention a rich background in the traditions and music of the past.

Flexible Leadership

As one might expect, some consistent features emerge out of these chapters. Firm, yet flexible, leadership appears to be essential if a church is to move together and avoid fragmentation. Possibly the most powerful dynamic which rumbles below the surface when change is in the air is the fear of division. The fear is not irrational either, for countless churches have suffered it. Yet despite mention of individuals leaving, our ten examples have all remained on the whole intact. In fact, the general impression is of a deepening of commitment and a growth in mutual respect rather than the reverse, as leaders have preached and prayed and talked and telephoned, and trusted that God was with them.

The chapters reveal leaders of great variety both in personality and styles of leadership, with and without musical ability or access to gifted helpers, and yet achieving equivalent success in the end. What they are not, however, are 'appeasers', who spend all their energy fending off murmurings of opposing pressure groups without giving a positive lead. Such methods will always reduce the leader to the role of piggy in the middle, until he finally catches the ball and changes the game.

Vision also emerges as an essential ingredient. A commitment to creating a Christ-centred, Word-inspired body of worshippers, creatively expressing the life of God within them, has to be held aloft through thick and thin.

Releasing Others

Those who encourage and make room for others to enter into ministry do far more for the body of Christ than those who dictate to others or use their brothers as a platform for the performance of their own talents. After all, the work of those with ministry gifts is to equip the saints for the work of service, not to impress the saints with their own work of service.

Towards this end, the appointment of music directors, or chief musicians, or in the case of dance, a dance group leader, is a consistent factor in releasing the creative potential locked up in the people. Over the years I have gained the impression, and I believe it is a correct one borne out also by these chapters, that only a minority of ministers and pastors include among their many gifts those associated with the creative arts. It seems that a certain kind of ministry releases a similar kind: the pastor brings forth pastors from his congregation, and the evangelist, evangelists. However, we see in these chapters a large measure of commitment to the practice of team leadership. For whilst the regular construction of a traditional 'hymn-prayer-sandwich' is easily within the abilities of a 'one-man-show' minister, the more specialised gifts of releasing people into Spirit-led worship, leading and training a music group, organising the extensive resources required to facilitate spontaneous worship, 'weighing' and responding to prophetic contributions and so on, may not be. In many of the churches, worship-planning groups have been formed, working under the leadership, and representing different areas of responsibility, from music through to banner making, facilitating more advance planning and better co-ordination of the 'ingredients' of the coming week's meeting.

Participation

There is a commitment to drawing as many as can participate to do so, and to training, encouraging, and 'initiating' those who as yet cannot. This includes children as well as adults, and recognises the potential in all who truly love the Lord to bring something of value to the whole fellowship. Participation is recognised as being not without its problems, as both natural and spiritual skills in bringing something of value to a public meeting need to be taught, nurtured and refined. It is also recognised that the invitation to participate publicly can give rise to a whole new set of challenges. There is the danger of certain persons trying a 'takeover bid', misguided people leading the meeting into confusion, folks mistaking a vivid imagination for divine revelation, or an individual with a point to make using the gathering as a platform to address publicly the whole fellowship via a prayer. Because of this, new skills have had to be learnt in sensitively steering, restraining and releasing, affirming the good and correcting the bad.

Flexible Structures

If any great suspension bridge is to survive, it must have flexibility built into its structure. A similar principle applies in these churches, and, of course, in the terms of the church, flexible structures only emerge where there are flexible people. Rigid service programmes have given way to more pliable ones, in some cases to large tracts of time where 'structure' is created on the spot. And it is interesting also to discover traditional liturgy co-existing happily with modern choruses. Of course, there have been those who believe that unless a Christian meeting is totally unplanned and spontaneous, then it cannot be Spirit-led. This belief, however, only results in the subtle emergence of an 'unwritten structure', where people's own habits and favourite songs regularly rise to the surface, and mediocrity and predictability creep in once again. A planned-and-prayed-over structure which invites the unexpected and unplanned seems to be the healthy balance between the two; a combination of prayerful, inspired advance planning, and 'on the spot' manœuvrability emerges as a workable solution, fuelled by the presence of active faith that the Holy Spirit will use the participants to guide, modify or interrupt. Of course flexible structures often require more components than rigid ones, and the resources required for free-flowing worship are vastly more than for programmed worship, if only from the perspective of musicians, who at the drop of a hat, may be called upon by a member of the congregation to accompany any one of five hundred popular choruses.

Desire for Reality in Worship

Worship is a great 'revealer' of the true state of a person's heart, which is one reason why such an apparently unthreatening activity can become the centre of so much strong feeling. All the church leadership represented here share a desire to be genuine in their practice of worship. They want the presence of God to be known among them, not just vain repetitions of words or songs, however true these words might be in themselves. The outward form without divine power is a sign of an apostate church, and all have longed for a deep inner transformation rather than outward 'cosmetic' changes. They have recognised the need for love and truth to be at the core—as in the early history of St Michael-le-Belfrey, where it was David Watson's teaching ministry which released the new life, which in turn overflowed into fresh expressions of praise and worship. The importance of good teaching and the centrality of the word of God are recurring themes, and are the major instruments used to create the structures of understanding within which liberty can be enjoyed, and the means by which the validity of both old and new practices are tested.

Notably, more worship has not necessarily led to less preaching; in fact, in some cases, preaching time has increased as well, leading inevitably to longer services. Despite the current tendency mistakenly to confine the use of the word 'worship' to 'a time of singing', the worship does not and should not stop when the preaching begins. Furthermore, if worship stops when the service ends, we are not meeting as true worshippers at all, since worship in its fullest sense is a way of life.

Cultural Relevance

Much of the motivation for bringing about change has been the concern that forms of worship should be made culturally accessible to the ordinary person. This is in no way a desire to pander to popular culture for the sake of being 'trendy', but a recognition that to the average person, much of what goes on inside churches seems 'coded' either in ancient language, or in more modern 'spiritual' colloquialisms that are mysterious to the uninitiated. In addition, if the music is alien to most people's experience, a further barrier is created. All our featured churches share a vision for evangelism, and as a result this issue takes on special importance when a steadily growing influx of new converts with negligible Bible knowledge or ecclesiastical experience is expected. Musical style needs to reflect the breadth of the people's tastes and backgrounds, and this of course will vary according to the nature of each church's catchment area. The worship needs to be simple, without being simplistic or bland; and in order to encourage people to be themselves, rather than adopting a peculiar Sunday service 'manner', a reverent informality needs to be introduced. People need to be encouraged to pray in their own words, complete with local dialect, rather than being made to feel that only a 'posh' voice and flowery biblical language are appropriate.

The Breaking of Old Patterns

This is of course implicit in almost everything that has been said so far. For every church, the process of change was accompanied to some degree by the sound of the creaking of old wineskins. Most report with sadness the departure of a few people who could not reconcile themselves to the changes, though by far the strongest impression is of the vast majority learning to worship alongside one another, in full acceptance of each other's differences. A fellow worship leader of mine commented recently how that whilst preferences can exist side by side very happily, prejudices cannot. It always warms my heart when I meet older Christians, who though they themselves find it difficult or impossible to participate in some of the newer expressions of worship, nevertheless encourage, fully support and pray for those who are pioneering the changes, recognising that God is at work. Notable in this respect is the church at Waltham Abbey, which against the background of an extraordinarily long and rich history, has gained great benefit from the creative tension between old and new forms of worship.

In terms of new patterns, it is interesting that a number of churches mention the period in the Old Testament after David brought the Ark of God to Jerusalem, as a useful 'model' for the organisation and practice of worship in the church. This era, recorded in I Chronicles 13:16–25 (see also Amos 9:11, 12; Acts 15:16), is seen as a foreshadowing of the church age, for the Ark was on public view to the worshippers; there was no veil, no blood sacrifices, and there was free access to every nation. Many of the Psalms were written during this period, and there was a strong prophetic ministry exercised on a large scale. The worship was massive and continuous, well ordered, organised and overseen. The fact that plenty of teaching is given around the Tabernacles of Moses, and by contrast most Christians do not even know that there was a Tabernacle of David, indicates that in the present climate much more attention could usefully be given to it.

Worship is a Relationship

One of the hazards of writing about the practice of worship is that whilst it is easy to describe the principles, planning, process and performance of it, it is very difficult to describe the experience. It is essentially something to be entered into, not something to be theorised about. Just like any human relationship, you cannot easily quantify it, but have to be part of it for it to make any sense to you. It is the difference between knowing, or just knowing *about*—the paraphernalia surrounding worship must not be mistaken for the thing itself, but as a means of helping us to enter into the heart of God.

Because true worship is the overflow of a relationship, and by virtue of the fact that we have been made partakers of the divine nature, an eternal one as well, there can never be a static arrival point in the process of it. A relationship which is static and unchanging is dead; thus if our experience of worship ever becomes tedious, boring or predictable and deadness sets in, we need to examine first of all the quality of our relationship with God before we leap to criticise the quality of our practices. It will doubtless be the experience of many, after disposing of the old written liturgy, albeit in many cases the 'hymn-prayer-sandwich' liturgy of the non-confirmists, that a new 'unwritten liturgy' begins to emerge. This threatens to become just as dead and restricting as the one that was replaced, not nearly as interesting as the unique talents of Cranmer made the Anglicans' liturgy to be. To worship God must be the consuming passion of the heart, whether we express it in old ways or new ways, in silence or with shouts, in stillness or with dancing.

We end where we came in, with the Samaritan woman at

Jacob's well. It is significant that her first act in her first few minutes as a 'true worshipper' was to gather her friends and neighbours, and breathlessly invite them to meet the person 'who told me everything I ever did'. The truth had set her free; the living water was beginning to well up within her, and she overflowed with the glories of Jesus. In the gathering momentum of these last awesome days, I believe that worship and the preaching of the Gospel are going to flow together as one powerful stream into the world, and the source of this powerful stream will be an ever deepening personal encounter, by the Spirit, with Jesus himself.

Chapter 1

The Abbey Church of the Holy Cross and St Lawrence Waltham Abbey, Essex

Colin Travers

Christians have worshipped at Waltham Abbey from Saxon times until the present. And in this atmosphere of revered history the church's vicar, Colin Travers, is well aware of both the seductions and the strengths of tradition. He writes eloquently of the tensions inherent in worship—tensions common to any body of worshipping Christians such as the struggle between old and new forms, between silence and shouting, between the needs of the individual and those of the group. He speaks of the delicate balancing act worship leaders must strive to achieve.

Colin read theology at Oxford and trained for the ministry at Ridley Hall. With his wife Joy, a social worker, he has two sons, Andrew and John. He enjoys keeping chickens and playing trains!

The Great Balancing Act

There has been a Christian presence in Waltham Abbey for well over a thousand years. Indeed, the story of Waltham Abbey Church is woven into the story of England. Founded in Canute's reign by Tovi the Dane to house a miraculous stone crucifix from Somerset; re-established by the last

Saxon King, Harold, who lies here; enlarged by Henry II in penance for the murder of Archbishop Thomas Becket; the Abbey saw most English kings down to Charles II. Some seeds of the Reformation were sown when Henry VIII was here with Thomas Cranmer in 1529. Although but a fragment of the glorious building raised soon after 1100, the Romanesque columns and arches, with the fine lady chapel built by the prosperous town just before the Black Death, the west front with its later tower, and the restoration last century by the talented William Burges—all make the Abbey epitomise English church architecture as it does our history. Here, then, is a church steeped in history and tradition.

Not surprisingly, though, the town of Waltham Abbey has changed and grown—not least in the past twenty years, during which time the population has trebled. A small market town of 6,000 people has mushroomed into a sprawling community of over 21,000. This has been largely due to development of three London overspill estates. The challenge that has faced the Abbey Church has been that of preserving a fine tradition of worship and music while at the same time responding to the needs of the present inhabitants, many of whom are not well acquainted with the choral works of Thomas Tallis—who was organist here at the time of the dissolution of the monasteries!

I came here as Vicar four years ago with the conviction that at a place like this, I had a duty and privilege to preserve tradition but also to enable today's people to worship freely and with a relevance and joy that would attract others to join. In setting about such a task I became aware of a number of tensions to be worked out. Embracing such difficulties has been painful, but the risk had to be taken. This is the high wire act of church: a great balancing act that can bring exhilaration and stimulation to worship, thus avoiding staleness or superficiality. In this chapter I shall set out a list of *tensions in worship* that must be considered and grappled with if creative worship that meets the need of the whole congregation is to be developed. I shall then outline how this works out in practice, highlighting some of the pitfalls and the pleasures.

The Tensions of Worship

The Old and the New

Tradition is important in worship. We should constantly remind ourselves that we stand in a long line of Christians who have worshipped down the centuries before us. Previous generations have left a rich heritage of music, of prayer and of liturgy that should not just be discarded, for it represents a distillation of the experience of God by his people of old. I often reflect, when worshipping in the Abbey, that those walls have witnessed countless acts of worship; here the rich and famous together with the poor and humble have offered their worship, day in, day out. Of course times change, language changes and customs change, but in this generation that regards everything as transitory and disposable I believe it vitally important not to forsake the bedrock of Christian tradition in our worship. But neither should those entering church for worship feel that they are entering a time capsule that swiftly projects them back a few hundred years and encourages them to imagine that God is a God of the past and not the present. The God who has been our help in ages past is also the God who is our hope for years to come. A healthy respect for the traditions of the past must go hand in hand with a keen desire to experiment with new forms and approaches.

The One and the Many

Then there is the real tension between the individual and corporate aspects of worship. We come to worship the Lord, not each other! Holding hands during the prayers or an interminably long interval for the exchange of words of peace can destroy the opportunity for the individual to enjoy a close encounter with Almighty God in one go. But to sit as far apart as possible in a vast church for the eight o'clock Communion hardly does much to enrich and enhance the quality of fellowship. Awareness of what is happening to the individual and to the whole group in any act of worship is essential.

Here and There

Linked with what I have just been saying is the tension between the transcendent and immanent elements in worship —between that which is beyond and that which is abiding with us. In a sense, where two or three are gathered in our Lord's name he is there in their midst. Yet in another sense, he is always beyond our ultimate grasp. He is here but not only here, so he bids us reach out for the vision of the heavenly country that begins here but ends beyond.

Silence and Shouting

In the Scriptures we are bidden to be still before the Lord but also to shout aloud his praises and clap our hands in joy. There is a danger today that our worship can become too busy and reflect the turmoil of our weekday lives. The charismatic revival has done much to enliven and brighten tarnished Anglican services, but we must be careful not to deafen the Lord Almighty with incessant incantations. Silence can breed the fertile atmosphere in which the Lord can truly and clearly speak to his people at worship and prayer together. There is a time to dance before the Lord and another to wait before him in silence. I can recall many a poignant silence following a rousing chorus.

The Veteran and the Novice

'I wish the vicar wouldn't keep giving out page numbers and treat us like imbeciles' is a cry that is often heard from those hardy worshippers of fifty years standing. But have you ever considered for a moment what it must feel like to cross the threshold of a church (especially an old Abbey!) for the first time in many years? Our worship must be inviting, as must our welcome at the door. Clear instructions that are not intrusive are essential if the newcomer is not to feel totally bewildered. Not only that, but there must be something for the first-timer to latch onto and engage with.

Heart and Head

A rounded faith and one of integrity will engage all the

faculties. We bring our whole selves to God in worship, and we need to give attention to what we feel, think and experience. Truly creative worship sweeps us up—heart, mind and body—to offer our very selves to God. Too long a sermon, twenty minutes standing on our feet, or repeating the same song three times can easily disengage one from what otherwise was a helpful and meaningful act of worship.

Waltham Abbey Worship

A creative balance is achieved when the tensions outlined above are addressed sensitively as worship is prepared. Very often we get it wrong, but just occasionally we sense— indeed we know—that the Spirit has truly moved, and we have been involved in real worship. We move now to consider how we at Waltham Abbey have tried, albeit inadequately, to put the principles above into practice. If you have found my comments so far discouragingly idealistic, I hope you will find the following encouragingly practical.

The Monthly Pattern

Over the years we have tried to devise a monthly pattern of worship that would provide all ages and types of people with an opportunity to worship in a meaningful way. Our principal service is on a Sunday morning at 10.30; on the first Sunday this is a family service, and on the other Sundays we have a parish Communion with the Sunday school meeting at the same time—though this is about to change to include a family Communion on the third Sunday, with the Sunday school only meeting fortnightly. In the evening at

6.30 there is greater variety. On the first Sunday we have a choral Communion, on the second a congregational Evensong, on the third a healing Eucharist and on the fourth a choral Evensong. When there is a fifth Sunday we usually have a specially devised different service in the evening. As with many churches we find that our attendance is far better in the morning than the evening. We usually number about 150 in the morning (with more at the family service) but only between 50 and 75 in the evening. I will describe these services in turn, trying to highlight some of the issues that arise from those tensions in worship already mentioned.

The Monthly Family Service

For some time this has been devised from scratch by one of two teams; these teams, who work with me or the curate, include musicians, Sunday school teachers and others with particular gifts in leading worship, speaking or acting. Originally there was only one such team, but we have found that sharing the work, with each team preparing only six services a year, has reduced the burden and meant fewer midnight sessions caused when ideas had dried up. Creative worship is rewarding to prepare and present but also extremely demanding. Each year we take a theme and build our series of family services around it. Recent themes have been 'The Parables', 'The Ten Commandments', 'The Prophets' and 'People Who Met Jesus'. At the planning meeting about three weeks before the service, we consider how we will tackle the subject for that month. Sometimes the ideas come quickly, but on other occasions we search and struggle for two hours or more. We are always looking for something that will be visually stimulating, something that will engage the children but speak to the adults as well; family services should not just be children's services.

We have found from experience that the services that really go well are those with plenty of active participation by the congregation, and those that last only about 50 minutes. Let me give you an example. Last Sunday the theme of our service, within our annual theme, 'Parables', was 'Pictures of Faith'. We took four word-pictures of the Kingdom painted by Jesus and recorded in St Matthew's Gospel: 'salt of the earth', 'pearl of great price', 'mustard seed' and 'leaven in the lump'. During the service we paid visits to our own *Blue Peter* studio to meet 'Peter Duncan' and Dr Heinz Beanz, who conducted a series of scientific experiments with children from the congregation. We thought about the properties of salt, the preciousness of real pearls and the life contained in a tiny seed or small piece of yeast. Mustard and cress were 'grown' during the service, and a huge plant grew out of the pulpit. These scenes were interspersed with the appropriate Bible readings and lively action choruses. I gave three short (two- or three-minute) talks on the difference our faith makes, the value of our faith and the power of faith. In that service the saying 'You are the salt of the earth' came alive for children and adults alike in a new way. The service had the merit of moving on from one activity to another after only a few minutes (before the children switched off), and the whole thing lasted 59 minutes. Apart from me, five other people were involved in leading the service, so change of voice was frequent. The music was led by our music group.

On the whole we would say that our family services are well attended and highly 'successful', but we are acutely aware of the fine line that exists between what is entertainment and what is worship. We are not in the circus or pantomime business! In addition to what is learnt at these services is—we hope—the all-important and infectious, relaxed and happy atmosphere in which families can experience that it is good—even fun—to worship together on a Sunday morning. We have discovered that the setting up of a team is essential, and that the team must include creative folk, some of whom are confident in leading. The organist or music group leader should be a member of the team as well. We try to keep the ideas simple and execute them crisply and with style. We see this family service as a shop window for the church, and through it we are hoping to attract new people inside as they commit themselves more fully to the worshipping life of the Abbey. In this we have not been very successful. There are a great many who come regularly on that first Sunday but are seldom seen at other times. One reason is the stark contrast in style that exists between the various services. But there is also some evidence that many folk just want to remain on the fringe, where the demands of commitment are not felt. It may be that family services of the type I have described encourage just that.

Family Communion

It is for this reason that we are shortly to introduce into our monthly pattern, on the third Sunday, a family Communion service. This will have an abridged and free ministry of the Word with teaching aimed at children as well as adults. Some of the more formal hymns will be replaced by songs and choruses, and wherever possible the children will be encouraged to take part. An attempt will be made to link this service with what is going on in Sunday school on the second and fourth Sundays.

In many churches there is quite a gap between Sunday school and church: sometimes to the extent that they might just as well be separate entities. It is most important for the children to feel that whether they are in Sunday school, family service or family Communion they are sharing in the life of the one church family. How many of us have met plenty of people who were *sent* to Sunday school but never darken the doors of a church today? The family Communion will obviously have some liturgical structure, but there is no reason why it should be dull. Indeed, children can respond to the drama and symbolism of the Eucharist and get caught up in the experience of a gathering of the Lord's people around his table. We intend to do quite a bit of teaching on what the Communion is all about during the first six months or so. This idea of family Communion has met with some resistance from our Sunday school staff, and the PCC needed some convincing, but I am sure that it is an essential part of church strategy to enable our children to be nurtured in the faith until they become fully committed adult Christians.

The Music Group

A music group was established at Waltham Abbey five years ago following the appointment of a new director of music. He was chosen for his wide musical sympathy and expertise. We are fortunate in having someone who is equally at home conducting Thomas Tallis or performing Betty Pulkingham. There is no doubt that without a musical leader of real talent and broad interest the development of creative worship is severely hampered. The director, together with his newly appointed deputy, is responsible for all the music in church; the two of them have a monthly meeting with the clergy to plan ahead. The musicians in the group play guitar, double bass, flute, synthesiser, piano and percussion and are sometimes accompanied by an organ. They lead us in a wide variety of singing including renewal songs and choruses and Taizé chants in Latin. For some time, when the music group played at services, they were viewed with some suspicion. I distinctly recall one member of the congregation disparagingly calling them the 'band' and others staying away 'when that racket was going on'. They have, however, now found a place of affection in the hearts of the congregation because of their high standard of musicianship and their undoubted Christian sincerity. Whatever we do, we must do it well and for the right reason—to glorify God. For too long worship in church has been to the accompaniment of piano or organ alone; the creation of a music group can release latent talent in the Christian community and bring a fresh liveliness to the worship.

Traditional Services

As this book is about new developments in creative worship I will not dwell overlong on the traditional services at the Abbey. I have already stressed the importance of tradition in worship and would emphasise that it is a great mistake to change everything just for the sake of change. We value our use of traditional church choral music and the liturgy of the church. In particular it can give rise to quieter moments of spiritual reflection. But can the traditional and the new happily live cheek by jowl in the same service? Great care must be taken, but the answer is YES. Quite recently we

were privileged to play host for the ordination of priests in
this part of the diocese. I had attended an ordination in the
cathedral a year earlier when my curate was made deacon.
I had felt that the music had been dull and inappropriate for
the occasion and so was determined that dullness should
not be repeated this year in the Abbey. The director of
music and I selected a blend of music ancient and modern
and agreed that we should have both the festival choir and
music group at the service. The service began with the introit anthem, 'I Was Glad' by Parry and ended with the as-
sembled 600 rejoicing in the words of the modern classic,
'Our God Reigns'. The blend was rich indeed, and many
commented on what an inspiring occasion it was. Dignity
can be achieved without dullness! A more homely example
is that of a recent praise evening held in the Abbey on a fifth
Sunday evening. In the midst of a service of jubilant praise
Tony—the curate—and I led a series of quiet contemplative meditations on the life of St Peter. Here contemplative
prayer and renewal music complemented one another in an
act of worship that engaged the whole person. We should
not be afraid to mix our own rich blend of worship.

The Healing Communion

This service was introduced in the autumn of 1985 on the
third Sunday evening each month. Within the context of an
especially quiet and unhurried service of Holy Communion, the sacrament of the laying on of hands is administered
to those who are sick or particularly troubled. In contrast to
our other services the musical resources deployed here consist of a solitary organist. The musicians enjoy a well de-
served evening off, and the service gains a quiet simplicity.

Everything on that evening is aimed at an atmosphere of stillness and peace with a minimum of distraction. The laying on of hands is ministered after counsel by the clergy at the altar rail. We have been greatly encouraged by the response to this service that obviously meets a need; when one is sick, bereaved or anxious, the main service can be overwhelming. Here is the justification for a service that takes the needs of such an individual very seriously.

The Great Balancing Act

I have tried to outline a picture of how we have developed our worship at the Abbey over a number of years. Despite its great history, Waltham Abbey is a very ordinary sort of place, and we seek not to be an imitation cathedral but a parish church serving the needs of the local community. In fact, having a very special building—glorious as it is—can have the disadvantage of creating a culture gap; the building itself can be threatening to those who are not appreciative of grand architecture. We have, therefore, had to work extra hard to convince folk that what goes on in our building can have a great relevance and meaning for their everyday lives. At the same time we have wanted to avoid the danger of our worship becoming banal or not worthy of God. It is a matter of imitating Jesus in meeting people where they are but taking them on further in their understanding and faith. Because people are all different in temperament, they will respond in differing ways to God in their worship. We must, therefore, strive for that creative balance that embraces many approaches and uses the varying gifts of the congregation.

Like the high wire act in the circus, leading and presenting worship will involve real risks, as we work with tension and try to achieve that perfect freedom of balance. It is indeed a great balancing act, but then we are worshipping a great God.

Chapter 2

Glenwood Church
Cardiff, South Wales

Robert Parsons

When Glenwood Church began in 1976, about a dozen people were meeting together, first in a home, then in a school. This group found itself in the middle of a massive metropolitan area (300,000 people), close to where the two great Welsh revivals of 1859 and 1904 had changed the whole country. As Rob Parsons comments, though, 'Memories are just about all we have left, and as a nation we love singing but not worshipping.'

Desiring to cater for the whole man, the group took the unusual step of building a sports centre rather than a church. Many have been attracted to this growing congregation. Worship here involves an emphasis on freedom, loving acceptance of differences, and openness.

Glenwood is served by four part-time leaders (two solicitors, an architect, and an electrical engineer), one full-time community evangelist and a full-time youth worker. Rob Parsons, one of the solicitors, is married with two children. His two hobbies are aged eight and five.

Glenwood in Context

This is not a chapter full of worship success stories; it is not in that sense a triumphant chapter. This is a chapter for all those churches teetering on the edge of a change in direction in worship but held back by fear of the unknown and the security of tradition. It is for those church leaders who, faced with the spectre of two groups in their church who want to worship differently and trying not to offend either, become transfixed like rabbits in the headlights of a car—unable to move forward or back and likely to be run over anyway.

When Graham asked if I would contribute to this book, I confess that the prospect daunted me in that I feel that by no standards is Glenwood yet a worshipping church in the sense that we have 'arrived'. I do however feel that we are on a journey; the most exciting part is that a body of people with very different ideas of worship are making the journey together.

It has never seemed to me a miracle that people with similar views on worship are found under one roof. It is no wonder that charismatics worship together or that those who hate raising their hands and dancing are all found in one church. That has never seemed to me to be evidence of the Faith. It may however be evidence that we are in Christ if a group of people who have quite different ideas about worship are prepared to stick with each other and move through the barriers which divide them. That will be costly. It may bring bitterness and difficulty; it will not be cosy, and we will find out if we really love even those who make us slightly uncomfortable in worship! If we cannot do this in worship—which is at the heart of our faith—we have no right to bring any message of reconciliation to a divided world.

I recognise the danger that at the end of our journey together we may all find ourselves sitting on a fence, and in an effort not to offend each other settle for something less than God really wants, but I do not believe that is necessary... Perhaps I should start at the beginning!

Glenwood Church is in Cardiff, a city of about 300,000 people, the capital of Wales. It is cosmopolitan. We are in the heart of a country that still remembers and is affected by three major Welsh revivals, in 1735, 1859 and 1904. Sadly, memories are just about all we have left, and as a people we love singing but not worshipping. We are therefore happy to sing hymns at a rugby ground, but there is deadness throughout much of our church life.

Glenwood in the Past

Glenwood Church began about ten years ago with a group of about a dozen people, meeting at first in a home and then in a school. It is on a housing estate of about twenty thousand people. When we decided to build we thought we should build a church to seat about 250 people. Then somebody said that to build a traditional church on such an estate was a 'cop-out'—a denial of the total needs of the area. It was suggested that what we needed was a sports complex where people could play as well as pray! As our minds raced round that idea we realised the need to cater for the 'whole man'—and for family life in a wide sense. We were moved by a comment of David Pawson in conversation: 'If you take a man's point of fellowship out of the pub, you have to give him a new one!'

With money in short supply we could not build both a traditional church and a sports centre, so we decided to

build the sports centre and to worship in it. We found we
could praise God in a gymnasium but not play football in
the middle of pews. We have never regretted our decision.

So we built a centre that had a five-a-side football court,
housing three badminton courts, men's and ladies' changing rooms, showers, coffee lounge and kitchen. It is certainly just as well that we pursued that course as the church
has grown so quickly that the originally planned accommo-
dation would have never held us. We are now often 400
plus, and we thank God that our gymnasium will hold seven
hundred and fifty.

When we came to consider our form of worship, we had
the advantage, being a new church, of a fresh start—although we were not naive enough to think we had a completely open mind. Many were from a Brethren
background with a good sprinkling of Anglicans, Baptists
and others, and we all came with theological cultures in
tow. There was, however, a genuine desire to be open to
God and to begin again.

Openness

In retrospect I believe we *were* prepared to be open, but
only within certain limits. Our worship highlighted that
dilemma. We somehow managed to produce two services
on Sunday which were like chalk and cheese. The morning
was an incredibly lively affair and the evening predictable
and often hard-going. If somebody had come into our evening service after having enjoyed the morning, he would
have found it hard to imagine it was the same fellowship. I
am sure that some found that service helpful, but many
found it quite an effort to take part in open praise or to feel

part of the worship. Some uninitiated in religious jargon dared to say they found it boring. The morning service grew in numbers and vitality while the evening service dwindled in both. How did we manage to get it so right at 11 am and so wrong at 6.30 pm? Perhaps I can pick out some of the elements which have been part of making that morning service such a successful one.

First, at the heart of the service's philosophy was the idea that people who were not used to coming to church were able to come into it without feeling threatened or ill at ease; at the same time we wanted them to experience worship which was both meaningful to them and us. We had all seen churches holding family services; however many of these were children's worship with adults sitting in. The preacher practically had to stand on his head to keep the kids' attention, and when it was all over, adults only said it was— 'nice'. We soon came to realise that such churches got the adults to attend only once in a while, on special occasions. They were then packed; the emphasis was usually evangelistic. However those churches rarely saw adults make commitments to Christ and had to keep special occasions going in order to get them in. Such churches usually had thriving Sunday schools and youth groups, and their philosophy was to bring the parents to Christ through the children. In practice it rarely happened.

We decided that our worship was to be adult worship (with children sitting in for part) and aimed for a consistency in music, drama and preaching. We were committed to reaching adults for Christ and—from there—whole families. We have found that to be a harder route, but much more fruitful than beginning with children.

That morning service did not have a directly evangelistic thrust. To a large extent it assumed that all had come to be part of collective worship. People from the housing estate just flocked to it, and one of the loveliest lessons that we learnt was that those who are not yet committed to Christ loved and needed to worship God. Many of them were in deep need in their personal lives—with family or marital problems, financial pressures, joblessness, and depression —but time and time again expressed joy at being able to be part of a worshipping church. We did not play down to them—we stretched their minds and spirits.

Worship at Glenwood

At the heart of our worship was systematic Bible teaching. We had few specifically evangelistic services. Instead we just worked our way through Scripture, and the distinction between evangelism and systematic teaching blurred as we began to discover the breadth of the Gospel of the Lord Jesus. People came to Christ almost weekly, and it was a surprise to many of us to see people become Christians in a non-evangelistic worship service. We had to learn to recognise responses to Christ with words other than 'I've accepted Jesus into my heart'. I will never forget a black lady with a strong Alabama accent saying 'I've found my religion again!'

Music was an integral part of our worship, and we fought against being stuck in a rut. We have an enormous number of musical gifts in the church, but they are of all kinds, from concert pianists to devotees of heavy rock. We use both! Part of the joy of that morning service is that the congregation never know musically what is coming next! With so many musical gifts we realise that musicians needed to offer their music to God as an act of worship. It was quite something for us to learn to appreciate a piece of classical music played as an act of worship even though it wasn't a recognisably 'Christian' tune. We have learnt to love music for music's sake. I believe it was so important that we learnt to tolerate each other's musical tastes, and I am quite sure that was a help to us when in later years we were going to have much greater tests of our tolerance than musical preference.

We made a particular effort to use people who were gifted in that service. That sounds a simple point, but many of us had come from the kind of background where everybody could 'have a go' in the pulpit. But that seemed to us to be a travesty; it would impose on the church people preaching without a real gift and would in fact stop those very people from discovering their true ministry. In addition, we quickly saw that it was necessary to have people leading those meetings who had a genuine ability both to make people feel at home and inject vitality into our worship. Morning services were structured, but only in the sense that they were led from the front. They were never predictable, rarely boring and with enough variety that even if the preacher had an 'off' day, the balance of the service made up for it.

Our Sunday evening services, though, were quite different. Although there were occasional high spots, by and large they were difficult meetings. I can best describe the form as Brethren-type breaking of bread meetings. There was no systematic teaching, and they consisted of open worship plus communion. In fairness I must say our premises did not help in open worship, and if there was any emotion it certainly did not come from the aesthetic benefits of worshipping in a gymnasium.

However, it was obvious that the lack of freedom in

worship was more fundamental than just physical re-straints. In retrospect it seems to me (and it *is* a personal view) that when we began at Glenwood we were prepared to be open minded on just about everything—architecture, the place of women in the church, evangelism—but when we looked at the kind of worship service that most of us had been used to, we were not prepared to change. We held the Brethren-type breaking of bread service as sacrosanct. The form of worship that we were used to for many years at 11 o'clock in the morning in a Gospel Hall was simply moved seven and a half hours forward to a sports hall. We had been flexible in everthing except that.

We tried just about everything to get life into that ser-vice. Eventually we changed the programme so that only twice a month we had that kind of open service, and on the other weeks a structured meeting. But the difference in worship and atmosphere between that and our morning service remained a mystery.

Pride—and Some New Lessons

However, we were proud of Glenwood. We told everyone we spoke to what a wonderful place it was, how successful evangelism was, what a wide variety of activities we had there—from working with the unemployed to a telephone counselling service. We told everybody that it was a loving church and full of joy. Then disaster struck us. There were difficulties in personal relationships; there was hurt, and suddenly both leadership and congregation were wonder-ing what had hit us.

To make matters even more complicated, in the middle of those issues we reached in our evening teaching

programme I Corinthians 12, 13, 14 and began to consider
some of the gifts of the Holy Spirit and their relevance to
our church. It is probably difficult enough facing the charismatic issue when life in other areas is reasonably quiet, but
we came to face it in a church that was already feeling vulnerable.

So far as anybody could remember nobody had ever spoken in tongues or prophesied in Glenwood, and each of us
came to that teaching with a degree of trepidation. We
ended those weeks of teaching believing as a church that
those gifts were for today, but subject to the restraints that
Scripture places on them. We were open to God and desired to find out and do what the Bible said, but we were
children in these areas and were recovering from a period
of emotional upheaval. Many were confused and afraid. I
gave the teaching, and certainly all I wanted when it was
over was a quiet life for at least a year!

However, as we grappled with both the personal hurt in
the church and the doctrinal and practical issues of I
Corinthians, attitudes began to change. In many ways we
had learned humility as a church. We no longer boasted
about Glenwood. We no longer said that there was a fantas-
tic spirit of love amongst us. We felt the need of God's grace
and help as never before. We called a half day of prayer and
just cried out to God for his mercy upon us. We were
brought very low that he might lift us. We discovered that
the love we'd talked so much about was now being tested,
and as a matter of practice we now had to work through towards forgiveness and reconciliation. Part of the fruit of
that hard experience was a little word of prophecy (one of
the very first) that said—the winter is over and the spring is
here.

There are two elements that every church has to face

when a body of people who have different views about worship (especially the charismatic versus non-charismatic) are together: fear and frustration. One part of the church is afraid to go forward—suspicious, and armed with a hundred-and-one horror stories—the other half frustrated because of the lack of freedom, often having to find expression for their worship in gatherings outside their local church.

A clear presentation of the church's doctrinal position is vital. This will highlight both the freedom and the restraints that Scripture has. Each member is brought under the authority of Scripture as the church works out practically what the Bible says. I believe that this does something for both fear and frustration. On the one hand if a church believes that the Bible teaches these things it also believes that the Father only gives good gifts to his children. This does not remove unease, but it attacks irrational fear. On the other hand, it helps those who feel frustration in worship because they realise that some of the things they have been looking for as essential indications of true worship are by no means either important or necessary in Scripture. At the same time they are encouraged to have an open attitude. Someone said to me recently that our leadership was open—and there is great hope for us in moving forward as a church in worship if that is so.

We did see a genuine change in attitude; this was most evident in the way our worship changed on a Sunday evening. We were learning to be tolerant of each other, learning to love each other and to put ourselves in the other person's place. One of the more profound ways in which this happened was that people stopped 'switching off' when the worship was different from that they were accustomed to; instead they admitted, 'Well, that wasn't quite my cup of tea, but I did hear God speaking to me through it.' In other words, there was fresh openness both to the Spirit of God and to each other. Thus we tried to encourage each other not to be so predictable in worship. Occasionally now the charismatics choose hymns from the old hymn book, and the others sometimes ask for a chorus to be sung twice!

The changes meant that people needed to be free to raise their hands, or to sit on them. It meant that we had to learn to respect periods of silence as equally worshipful as periods of prayer aloud. It meant that we had to learn to recognise when a prophetic word was being given, as well as being clear as to how we would test it. We decided in that area, for example, if somebody did have a word of prophecy that was going to affect the church as a whole, he or she should share it with the leadership first.

Another of the important lessons we had to learn as our worship became freer was that it is not necessarily the first thing that comes into your mind that God wants you to speak publicly. We learnt that 'The spirits of prophets are subject to the control of prophets' (I Cor 14:32).

As we moved on we began to see those signs of spring! In the past we had seen quite mature Christians making small protests in the evening service. Those who were not charismatic would refuse to sing choruses through a second or third time, and those who were would often sit with lips tightly shut when we were singing one of the old, favourite hymns. But then we began to experiment in both directions. We would occasionally use set prayers and also introduce some open worship into structured services. Slowly but surely one half of the church learnt not to be so afraid as we moved into uncharted waters, and the other half learnt at least to handle its frustrations in worship and to be patient as it believed God was teaching each of us his will and leading us on.

Freedom

More and more our worship together is becoming freer. I
do not mean by that that it is becoming typically 'charismatic'. There are words of prophecy and there is the occasional tongue; hands are raised and I think I even hear clapping; but I do believe we are learning too that some of the
more traditional forms of worship—such as older hymns,
periods of silence, formal prayers—are valuable and helpful. Loving each other means understanding each other,
being patient and bringing what we can to God. The irony
is, perhaps, that we are now going back more and more in
our evening service to the form of open worship and communion that we struggled so much with at the beginning—
but it seems to have a new freedom. Perhaps our lesson has
been that form is not half as important as attitude and openness to God himself.

One of the most fundamental lessons we learnt was that
the secret of real freedom in open worship is strong leadership. The leaders had to be prepared to encourage worship
and bridle excesses. On one occasion after one of the leaders had asked somebody to hold what she considered to be
a prophetic message until we could talk to her privately
about it, the whole church felt more secure. A leader rarely
now steps down from the pulpit when open worship is taking place, and we have learnt that to oversee is vital.

We do want to be part of a church that worships God. We
do want to be in a church where all of the gifts of the New
Testament are evident but equally with the constraints that
the New Testament puts on the exercise of those gifts. And
we do want to be part of a church that has a body of people
together who do not all worship in the same way.

We do not believe that God has called us to build a

church made up of 'concrete blocks' who all have to worship identically. We *do* believe God has put a pile of rough stones together who by his grace can learn to love each other, forgive each other, and worship with each other. Some say that we will yet have the splits that have occurred in so many fellowships; by God's grace that will not be so. We pray that we may be open to him, and receive from him the grace to hold all that is best from the past, guard all that is good in the present, and follow him into the future into the worship that he wants and deserves from each of us.

It cannot, though, just be a matter of getting two different groups to worship together; that would be wonderful, but it is not enough. What we must create is a spirit of openness to God so that he may actually be able to achieve what he wants in our churches—and perhaps surprise all of us.

The wind of his Spirit blows where he wants. By God's grace may he breathe through our church—and blow through our worship!

Chapter 3

Newhills Parish Church Bucksburn, Aberdeen

Norman Maciver

Coming originally from a strict Calvinist background on the Hebridean Island of Lewis with its centuries old tradition of metrical psalm singing in Gaelic, Norman Maciver now finds himself the pastor of Newhills Parish (Church of Scotland) Church in a rural area about six miles from Aberdeen. As he says himself, he has moved a long way from the days when he first anticipated full-time ministry. The one-man ministry typical of many Church of Scotland churches is not found at Newhills, where Norman is supported by Bruce McKenzie, a part-time minister, by Morag Elder, director of music and by four others.

Newhills enjoys a variety of worship both formal and informal, with a regular celebration of the Lord's Supper and an emphasis on pastoral ministry to both adults and children.

Norman is married to Irene, a nurse who works with handicapped children. Their four daughters, including twins, are now grown up. As a family they enjoy being with other people and travelling.

Congregational Heritage

Down through the centuries and across the nations, people
have with deep sincerity and passion given vivid expression
through their experience of their gratitude to God, who
loved them and loves them still. In the Presbyterian Church
of Scotland, John Calvin by his teaching exercised great influence, an influence that can be seen still in both the form
and content of worship. He followed Luther into a conviction that worship, to be truly authentic, had to be in the
worshipper's own language. Also, the form and content of
such an experience had to come under the control of Scripture, so central to worship was the unfolding of the trea-
sures of Scripture. It followed from this that any contemporary expression of Scripture, be it creed or hymn, was
essentially inferior. Therefore, in corporate praise, only
metrical versions of the psalms were permitted. In one
sense, an unfortunate consequence of this rediscovery of
the centrality and authority of the Word was that the whole
business of faith became more and more cerebral, increasingly a matter of understanding and knowing. At a stroke,
external aids became less and less acceptable. Musical
accompaniment, dramatic presentation, visual artistic
beauty, as time passed, became spiritually questionable.
Church buildings became austere and plain, and musical instruments were forbidden in worship.

It was exactly into this environment that the congregation of Newhills was born in 1662. An architecturally plain,
crisp building was constructed on a windy hilltop some six
miles from the already significant port of Aberdeen. It
served a scattered, developing community totally depend-
ent on agriculture for its livelihood. The original building
was subsequently altered to incorporate a small gallery, but

because of continued growth, the congregation was led to raise, close by, a new building that in those days was large enough to accommodate every resident in the parish. It had a seating capacity of more than one thousand. Built in 1830, it was still untainted by any extreme artistic endeavour. The windows were plain glass, and the singing of the still mandatory psalms and paraphrases was unaccompanied except that the precentor who led the praise had the starting aid of a tuning fork.

And so it continued in worship until 1945, and from all accounts the growing community was warm in its response. Before World War II there was a choir of more than 30 at Newhills, and the last precentor is recorded as having said that the church was noted for its congregational singing. This same precentor believed the human voice to be at its most beautiful in unaccompanied singing, and because of that he says, 'I am sorry to think that this traditional part of the religious service is passing away.' And so the 'kist o'whistles' (an organ) was installed to aid the praise of God in worship in this rural parish church. There are those still worshipping week by week in our fellowship who recall with an honest degree of heartfelt nostalgia, and yet with conviction, that these were days of authentic and pleasing worship, and who would dare question such an affirmation? Nevertheless, the last 40 years have seen significant changes in the form and style of worship in this same congregation, and perhaps the mark of its contemporary authenticity is that in spite of the real differences, our nostalgic reminiscers still find reality in today's varied expressions of worship.

Present Ministry

As its present minister I believe it is important for me to share something of my own background and thus to offer a more adequate understanding of the developments in our worship—if only to reveal the pain that sometimes affects us in change. It would be quite wrong to give the impression that the various changes in the expression of our worship have come about without such pain or without big questions on the part of the congregation and in the heart of its leadership. It is always vital in any development process that those who lead be aware of their responsibility to temper innovations with sensitivity; yet it is also true that progress through the wilderness as Israel journeyed to the Promised Land took place not when the pillar of cloud and fire was in their midst, but rather when the glory of God moved elusively beyond. So graciously the Lord had to deal with my own heart in preparation for all that he was to reveal to me in later days.

My own theological and cultural heritage lay in the very strict Calvinism of the lovely Hebridean Island of Lewis. I was reared on the mystical, haunting beauty of unaccompanied Gaelic psalm singing, worshipping as a boy in what was a somewhat austere church building. Still today, even though the Scottish mainland culture asserts its own increasing pressure, worship continues in the ancient language of the Gael. And so it ought to be—Calvin would have approved! Developing Calvinism in the Hebrides reacted vigorously against anything that tasted vaguely of worldliness, anything that gave the individual human personality encouragement for overt expression. The whole area of musical instrumental expertise, expressive literature and creative visual art was abandoned to the realm of the world; it smacked too much of the flesh and was excluded from the activity of worship.

Side by side with this, a high doctrine of ministry is held in these islands with the clergyman being set apart from and indeed in many ways set above his people so that an awesome distance developed between clergy and laity. It should be remembered that the constitution of the Church of Scotland strengthens the clergyman's hand of control by giving him total responsibility for what happens during the time of worship.

Although from early teenage years I no longer either lived or worshipped in that culture, yet my boyhood experience left its mark on my life. When eventually the Lord led me into full-time ministry and called me into my present and only pastorate in Newhills, it was as one who saw his future committed to this style of one-man ministry. Yes, in the intervening years I had grown accustomed to singing hymns to the accompaniment of great organ music and on occasion even to guitars, but every departure from my childhood practice had to be examined most carefully and initially treated with suspicion, and this I find still to be true.

Thanks be to God, he has all things in his hands, and here in Newhills he has dealt with us graciously, leading by his Spirit step by step along the road to a fullness of experience in worship that 10 years ago I could never have anticipated. Jim Graham records how in his experience of the ministry of the gifts of the Spirit, the Lord dealt with him slowly, and so it has been in my own case here in Newhills in the development of worship. He has done this in our understanding and in the physical environment of worship, gently calling us back to a new appreciation of body ministry, raising up and leading personnel with specialist gifts and committed hearts, opening up new avenues along which we walk—at times tentatively—so that from week to week we learn new lessons. We are persuaded that his Spirit is alive and at work in our midst, and of course this causes us to rejoice more and more in his great love and fills our worship with enthusiasm and thanksgiving.

But we must be more specific about these experiences of God's grace because they touch every area of the life of our congregation. I emphasise that this account is of how the Lord is dealing with the situation at Newhills, with our hearts and lives; it is not necessarily the method he adopts with all others, nor is he restricted in how he will work in our midst in the coming days. We are on a journey with Jesus, led to him by the Spirit, and we would not dare to define the various steps on the road. Rather we look forward with expectation, anticipation and excitement, for we believe he will yet do greater things in our midst.

Buildings Matter

There is much evidence in the history of the Church that buildings can be designed in such a way as to contribute significantly and sympathetically to an experience of worship. In the building plan for the tabernacle, God gives instructions that will help the worshipper to experience both the presence and the nature of God (Exod 25:8ff), but so too there can be features in a building that interfere with the worshippers' appreciation of God and can hinder their experience of the presence of God. It might be a salutary exercise for the leadership in every fellowship if, instead of accepting that the building they have is essentially helpful for worship in every facet—simply because it is there in its present form—they reassessed its construction to see whether it encouraged authentic worship for today's people. Circumstances change, resources are important, and it is only wise stewardship to examine carefully from time to time the circumstances in which we are called to serve and to be convinced that our resources are most effectively deployed. So it was in Newhills.

In the late 1960's a considerable area of the parish that it had served faithfully over the three centuries suddenly became suburban. Although the church building itself was left in its splendid isolation, less than a mile away an attractive and desirable housing development grew up that made provision for a considerable influx of people of all ages, many of them with young families. My immediate predecessor applied himself to the pastoral care of these souls with considerable devotion and enthusiasm, and that, coupled with his gifted biblical preaching, was used by the Lord for the growth of the church family. Very quickly this taxed the existing building resources of the congregation, and, responding to a dream vision, the pastor led his people to the conversion of an almost derelict stable complex, which last century housed the minister's livestock and gig. A most valuable resource that has an environment of informal comfort, designed to encourage an atmosphere of deep worship of the Lord, was the result.

Today we still find that God is in the business of vision. As I write, we are being most encouragingly led into a substantial extension to the ancillary facilities beside our church. We pray that under God this vision will become a reality sooner rather than later with the construction of a new suite of purpose-built halls and rooms. Again, one of the controlling features of the design will be suitability as regards the worship of God. Our God is a faithful God, and our desire is to follow where he leads.

However, we must go back to 1978 for what has been one of the most significant building alterations affecting our worship. About 18 months after my arrival as minister, during a building inspection of the sanctuary, it was discovered that some of the joists under the floor were structurally unsound. Although professional advice suggested that their replacement was not urgent, the Kirk Session decided to remedy the situation quickly. This of course meant the removal and demolition of the existing pews, which left the leadership with a straight choice; either the pews could be reinstated, or some other seating arrangement had to be used. After considerable thought and prayer, the pews were replaced by movable stacking chairs. By that single action the whole atmosphere of worship was changed. It would be utterly presumptuous to claim that this decision and the response to its implementation were accepted with unanimous approval. There were many who doubted its wisdom, and even eight years later there are still a few who feel that the church has been spoiled. It is certainly less 'churchy', but the vast majority are in no doubt about the great benefits of this structural change. We have both flexibility and informality and both have contributed significantly to a new excitement and relevance in worship. There is opportunity for greater movement of worshippers throughout the church, especially in the half hour before the services begin, and at the close of the service all are invited to share in a time of fellowship with coffee served in the sanctuary. Those who worship together are encouraged by the whole environment of the building to relate to one another and to appreciate one another in the Lord's family. God as Father is becoming more real in our experience because the physical environment in which we worship him is drawing us closer together and thus enabling us to express more adequately our unity as brothers and sisters in Christ. There is no doubt that we have seen again the positive contribution that the physical environment of worship makes to the expression of the believing community's devotion to their Lord and Saviour.

Importance of Music

As already indicated, there was in former years a strong singing tradition in the congregation, and although in recent years we have been served in this area by a succession of able and dedicated organists, during my own ministry, in spite of various endeavours, there was little development in this important part of the worship of God. Certainly the congregational praise was impressive, the organ accompaniment excellent, but there was no great variety, and clearly the musically gifted in the congregation had little opportunity to use their individual gifts in the worship of God. Nevertheless, the Lord was preparing one or two chinks of light and almost a dull glow of life to be fanned in his time into a dancing flame of song and praise; for example, one or two members of the congregation were led to compose songs of worship which we sang to well-known Scottish tunes. The seeds for this had been sown as far back as the last service of worship in church before the removal of the pews. On that Sunday, the praise was led by a group who played professionally as a Scottish dance band, one of our own elders being one of their number. All the praise items during that service were sung to popular Scottish tunes.

Then in 1981 we began to hold for a week or two each

summer in a field opposite the church an open-air mission for children and young people, with the facility to move into a sanctuary area, now carpeted and cleared of chairs, if the weather was less than kind. Although our own membership provided the leadership for these missions, musically we were restricted and found we had to depend on outside help. These times were blessed by the Lord, and most meaningful contacts were made with many families in the parish.

In 1983 we were asked as a congregation to participate in the training programme for a trainee deaconess. She worked with us for some 10 months, and while she did many valuable things, she will long be remembered for her beautiful singing voice. During her time with us she contributed greatly to the worship of God through her most moving ministry of song, and in addition as a guitarist she led us in new worship choruses.

The following year we had a mission beginning on the Sunday with a service of commissioning, and on the previous evening we were still without a guitarist to lead the open-air chorus singing that had become such an important part of the children's worship time each morning. We had prayed and enquired about help, but to no avail. And then it happened! One of our elders, our first student in many years for the full-time ministry, was visiting that evening in another area of town, and he and his wife shared the church's concern about the music for our mission. Also visiting that home was a young music graduate, a girl who loved the Lord, and who offered to help us out.

God had answered our prayers, and he had opened for us a doorway that led into pastures far richer than we could have ever imagined. Our organist at the time had already expressed the desire to resign because of family commitments, and six months after her first offer of service that same music graduate became our organist and now is our minister of music. Furthermore, as a consequence of these days of summer mission, our young folk began to learn many new songs of praise, and gradually we were able to introduce these into our normal worship services, mostly to organ accompaniment. The light was beginning to dawn gently and new possibilities were ahead of us. Truly the hand of the Lord was upon us.

Over these past two years there has been a number of significant developments in our music ministry. This young lady has gathered together a mixed group of about 20 people and has gently moulded them into an enthusiastic and accomplished singing team. Early in their life together they felt they wanted a name by which they could be identified. A number of suggestions was made, but no decision had been taken. Their first public ministry was an informal service at a local sheltered home for the elderly, and that evening I preached on the text 'Jesus exhorted the people and preached good news to them' (Luke 3:18). One of the names being considered was 'Good News', and so they are named. Being herself an accomplished violinist and guitarist, the leader began to offer guitar instruction, and today there are about 10 of our own members learning and playing guitar week by week in our services of worship. Gradually we began to discover that in response to her leadership many who had musical gifts in the fellowship offered to help, and now on a regular basis we have a twenty-member orchestra leading the praise in the sanctuary.

Things still continue to develop. Through the vision of a recent member of the church and with our music minister's help and guidance, a strong male voice group has been born and is beginning to exercise a powerful ministry to the glory of God. Even as this story is being recorded a small group of young gifted musicians has drawn together to form a gospel rock group.

But these developments have not been confined to the area of music. The wider sphere of body ministry is being motivated as members of our fellowship are being released to exercise their ministry in music. The Lord has touched the hearts of others artistically gifted for ministry and is leading them to use their own particular gifts. Sacred dance has featured in occasional services, although my own Calvinist heart thumped a bit more vigorously at the very thought of this. It need not have done so because the Lord used this group to minister most movingly, particularly during an Easter celebration of praise. Also, there are stirrings about the possibility of gospel banners in the near future. We are being very careful to stay close to the Lord in all this, being only too well aware of the temptation to move from an authentic experience of worship to a weekly parade of talent—religious entertainment. Our criteria for any activity in a service of worship are clear. It must be a necessary part of the whole service, there being no place in worship for artistic expressions for their own sake. There is also a deep desire that those involved come from among the active members of the congregation. In other words, we are beginning to understand and experience in worship the body ministry that Paul urges in his Epistles. This means that while we exercise our gifts with as much competence and expertise as we can, so too there must be an avenue for all who feel led to minister. Our concern is that in worship we offer all that is best to our Lord who gave everything for us, but each worshipper must be free to participate in that offering.

We know from the Scriptures that the temple had many musicians, whereas in our Presbyterian tradition we confine ourselves almost exclusively to one organist and a few choir members, with the adventurous occasional couple of guitarists. It has become clear to us that it is only as we recognise the significance of a ministry of music by appointing musicians that more people are encouraged to recognise their own God-given gift of music. We are discovering that we are moving away from the attitude that enjoys the 'performance' to that place where we understand it as God ministering to us through his gifted messengers.

A consequence of this is a congregation which more effectively offers its worship to God. In the spiritual life of the church these new, developing ministries find their true importance since it is the whole body that is the gauge of growth, not the length of a toe or a finger. Thus people ministering in an individual way should come out of, but not preclude, an active praising congregation. Each contribution to worship must be part of our experience of God and must also be in a form that we can comfortably employ. We are careful to ensure every age group in our congregation is enabled to participate in our worship life. The young are involved in specific family services, many of them leading worship, and a recent development has been a shortened celebration of the Lord's Supper, designed particularly to meet the needs of the elderly and infirm. Always the words and actions used must be relevant to where we are today. All this has meant a growing repertoire of praise that we believe is pleasing to our Lord.

One Body, Many Parts

Important as the development of praise is in worship, it is
never the whole of worship, and we are deeply grateful to
God for the way in which his Spirit has led us in these last
years into a new experience of shared ministry. This has
created a climate in which the variety of gifts just referred
to has been warmly accepted in our growing congregation.

It will be remembered that as the product of my own
heritage, I came into full-time service with a very jealous
understanding of ministry. It was mine to exercise, maybe
even delegate in part, but I had never—either in my experience or in my theological training—been guided into a truly
biblical examination of that ministry. However, as my own
ministry developed, I discovered that there were those in
the congregation with considerable spiritual gifts, and as I
searched the Scriptures, I began to see that these gifts had
to be released in the service of the Lord for the strengthening of his body. Gradually, through sharing in small ways in
the leadership of public worship, leading informal small
groups, being encouraged to speak in services for old
people, giving testimony in the open air, there began to
grow in the life of the congregation a biblical understanding
of ministry so that today every service has multiple leadership and I can be released by the congregation from time to
time knowing that the leading of worship is in excellent
hands. This is quite unusual in the Church of Scotland where
the conduct of worship is in the hands of one person who is
generally the ordained minister—although in addition certain categories are approved by the General Assembly. Significantly, not even ruling elders are included. Over the
years we have seen individuals grow in spiritual stature,
moving from a tentative brief reading to spiritually powerful

expositions of God's Word as they have gained in confidence and been drawn closer to the Lord. It is also a matter of sheer joy for us to see in these days our own Church of Scotland examine with deep concern the traditional expression of ministry and being led to say:

> That the Church is the Body of Christ radically undermines any instinct to elevate the calling and ministry of some above others, since all the members of the Body are equally subordinate to Christ, its own Head (Eph 4:15f); but it is also positively to affirm the ministry of every member, since each part of the Body, though different and distinct, is vital to the functioning of the whole.[1]

Furthermore, in our fellowship this has meant a growing desire for more worship opportunities so that in the summertime we have an additional morning service, and at the beginning of 1985 the Kirk Session decided to institute a weekly evening service, where previously it had been held monthly. Truly, God is working in fresh ways in our midst, and we are discovering new freedom in our times of worship so that we are able to affirm with Jacob 'Surely the Lord is in this place' (Gen 28:16). Where we differ from Jacob, however, is that we know it by his Spirit. These evening services are informal and in recent months have been blessed as we have shared informally round the Lord's Table and have been given opportunity to pray as individuals together, thus ministering to each other's needs. 'The Lord has done this, and it is marvellous in our eyes' (Matt 21:42).

A Growing Future

There is still much room for new experience; there is still a great distance to be travelled, but we are on the road and the Lord is with us. Our continuing conviction is that all that we do and say must agree with the Word of God and must have contemporary relevance. The preaching and teaching of the Word are still—as they were in the Reformation Church and always will be—central to our experience of worship, because no worship experience could be real except there is a word from the Lord to his people. Worship is that expression of a relationship of love, and through it God speaks in love. We are continually humbled that he, wonderful in glory and majesty, should deign to use us and our resources as instruments of his saving grace. My own desire has always been that those who come to worship should be comfortable when they are there, but uncomfortable for having been there; I want them to feel at home, yet challenged and changed.

We are at present on an exciting section of the journey with God, and because the worship of God cannot be isolated from the witness of his people in the world, so we expect growth and blessing in our witness. As the future lies before us, so the Lord has given us a vision not simply to participate in worship and be satisfied, but to go out into the world, and we are increasingly discovering that the relevance and power of God in worship is changing lives. In the past five years God has called three of our members into full-time missionary service overseas; five of our members are in various stages of training for the ordained ministry of the Church, and a number of others are exercising a devoted ministry for the Lord in hospital, school and Christian organisations.

Within our own fellowship a team of ministers, one full-time and six part-time, has been set apart, covering the areas of teaching, pastoral care, youth, music, Christian education and children. In training are those to be appointed shortly as pastoral assistants in the congregation, and they are to be followed by a team of trained evangelists for continuous parish visitation. In the past 10 years the membership of our congregation has increased from 850 to 1,050 and our weekly attendances are increasing steadily—all in a period when the total membership of our parent Presbytery has slipped back. Yes, we still have our problems: bridging the gap between large membership and smaller attendance; encouraging commitment in our members—but the very existence of these problems enables us to move on and to experiment rather than to become self-satisfied. And through them we are humbled to discover the gracious love and mercy of the Father.

We look to him to lead us on, convinced that he has still greater things in store for us. We will seek prayerfully to be obedient to the heavenly vision because our desire is that our Lord be glorified in all that we do. Our God reigns and has done mighty things, and it is our deep privilege to come and celebrate what he is still doing, who he is, and how much we love him. He brings his people together to delight in his presence. We gather as a big family; our Father speaks to us; Jesus by his Spirit ministers to us. As we grasp and are consumed by the excitement of this understanding of worship, then we have much to sing and dance about—joy, peace and love in our Lord. This is Good News. Truly 'we shall go out with joy and be led forth with peace'. Hallelujah!

Note

1 *Ministry: An Interim Report*—Church of Scotland Panel on Doctrine, General Assembly Report 1985.

Chapter 4

Ansdell Baptist Church Lytham St Annes, Lancashire

Andrew Dodd

Between the small towns of Lytham and St Annes near Blackpool, Ansdell Baptist Church attracts a growing congregation. Ministering to a community consisting of retired people, holiday-makers, and professionals from local and national companies, Ansdell has witnessed many changes both in its worship and work since its founding in 1904.

Not content to rest in the past, this church and its leaders are moving into new areas of worship, particularly in music. Members meet at the church twice on Sundays but spend all other worship times together in house groups. Worship is a relaxed mixture of liturgy and free-flowing forms.

Ansdell and its two 'daughter' churches are served full-time by John Austin, part-time by Iain Dunbar, and by a team of five elders. When Andrew Dodd, author of this chapter, is not occupied in his duties as co-music director with his wife Kathie, he is a solicitor and the father of two children.

Ansdell Baptist Church is situated between the small towns of Lytham and St Annes on the Fylde Coast south of Blackpool. Essentially a middle-class area with a large proportion of the population now retired, it does however accommodate locally major employers such as British

Aerospace, Guardian Royal Exchange, and Premium Savings Bonds, as well as a large holiday industry during the summer months.

Ansdell's History

The church was initially set up in 1904 on the edge of what was then the populated area. Because of new development, however, it now stands in a strategic position in the community, surrounded by a concentration of good housing and on a major road between the two towns. The church has gone through a number of changes over the last 25 to 30 years, from being a largely social church to an evangelical church, thereafter experiencing charismatic renewal and entering the mainstream of the renewal movement. The church has always maintained, and intends to continue to maintain, its links with the Baptist Union and is well linked with other Baptist churches of 'like mind' throughout the country, receiving from outside the support and encouragement of Douglas McBain on a regular basis.

Turning to recent history, during which the biggest changes have come, we can point first of all to the years 1972–1973 when there was a large influx of young people into the church as a result of the evangelical ministry of a group called Canaan who essentially spurred the introduction of a more contemporary form of worship into the church. Also in 1973 Nigel Wright joined us as pastor. He remained throughout the thirteen years of growth, having joined us straight from Spurgeons College, and has only recently left. The church and Nigel have moved on in pilgrimage together.

In those early years when the young people were growing

in number and experience, they held meetings Monday and Friday evenings and also an after-church 'rendezvous' in local homes, where open prayer, praise and worship were usually led by one or two guitarists. The presence of the Lord was strongly felt on these occasions. Church services still however retained their traditional 'hymn-prayer-sandwich' structure. Despite the positive aspects of this form of worship, it was under pressure. The church was filling with new Christians, both young and old, and people were no longer satisfied with the older forms because they allowed little room for freedom of expression or for a sense of the presence of God among his people.

In 1977 new vision for worship came out of *Come Together* —the Christian musical by Jimmy and Carol Owens. As the young people met together to plan special events and new services using the music and worship like *Come Together*, a new freedom came into the services themselves. Two of the youth leaders in the church (Andrew and Carol) were discussing the experience of worship in the church, comparing it with what they had enjoyed with the *Come Together* choirs, and the Lord spoke to both at the same time. They wondered why the excitement of *Come Together* worship was only outside the church, not inside their own church every week. *Come Together* choirs had generally sung outside church worship services and there was a tremendous sense of frustration that the freedom that had been found in the musical was not being regularly experienced within the weekly church gathering. Armed with a new vision, they experimented with various groupings of younger people and their leaders, at Christmas and at Easter and at other meetings—leading singing of worship songs and ministering in song. The first times of ministry were pretty rough: the church sound system was for speech only, and there were not enough microphones to go round, a common experience of many churches. (Since then our sound system has been renewed and now operates on a professional level.)

The group that was formed out of those times took on the name 'Habitation', which was intended to convey the fact that God inhabits the praises of his people (Psalm 26:8). Before being used in the regular services of the church, however, the group worked independently for some months, building strong musical and spiritual foundations. This was in an effort to ensure that when change came, it would have more chance of being of a permanent quality.

Music at Ansdell

In those early days our times of free-flowing worship and praise were limited, perhaps just a block of two or three songs placed in the middle of the traditional service. The group often wrote and sang ministry songs which would be used to encourage the people or support the message. The composition of the group did not consist entirely of young people—in fact it was quite a mature group. We found great strength in this small grouping of people who were to see through the early days of revival of our worship together. The commitment of the members of the group was vital not only to the ministry in the church but to the members themselves. Prayer and worship together was invaluable, for out of those times came the joint strength and vision to 'see us through'.

One of the tools we found useful in encouraging renewal within the church was praise and prayer meetings, which were held perhaps on a Friday or Saturday night with a guest speaker. There our worship was easier and flowed more freely. These meetings were open to any members of the church and served as a learning forum not only through the teaching received but also through meeting together as brothers and sisters in a more informal atmosphere. These meetings were a gentle introduction to the freedom the Holy Spirit could bring in our worship, a better alternative to forcing a radical change in the church services. Those who were interested were free to come and go as they pleased. In this learning environment people became stronger in the Lord, and more and more convinced that freedom had to come to our worship.

Movement into newer forms of worship and to the practice of gifts, such as prophecy, words of knowledge, encouragement, tongues and their interpretation, started in the evening services, which were generally less formal than the traditional morning service, and indeed where more young people were present. Our adventures started there, and our development has continued since those early days through a gradual evolution of our meetings so that they now contain far more worship songs than hymns. We arrange our worship in an almost continuous flow of music, leaving spaces as appropriate to allow the Holy Spirit to speak in his many ways or for people to encourage the body in prayer and prophecy. At times there is stillness and contemplation. There is in fact now very little difference between morning and evening services—the only constraint being that of time in the mornings, when we still wish to keep our services to one and a half hours because of the children. The evening services last longer—perhaps two and a half hours, but few children attend them.

One influence upon us in recent years has been the Vineyard teams from Yorba Linda and Denver, headed by John

Wimber and Tom Stipe. Two visits from the Vineyard
Ministries have brought an experience of worship and intimacy with God into our meetings which was not previously
there. As a result our experience of the Lord is much
deeper and wider both as a body and individually in worship. Their ministry to us changed our perception of worship in that they were somehow more relaxed, not crashing
into God's presence attempting to gain his favour, but
simply and boldly coming into the presence of a loving
Father who wanted to share his love with his children. Their
songs, stressing his abiding love for his people, were a
superb vehicle for expressing this, being simple and yet
heartfelt. Songs like 'Change My Heart, Oh God' and
'Come Let Us Worship and Bow Down' had a particular
ministry at that time. Hence our services now generally follow the pattern of open praise and worship; followed by an
opportunity for people to contribute and encourage from
Scripture, or with prophecy, words of knowledge, and testimony; followed in turn by preaching and a response to the
preaching in worship and praise. It is in these worship times
that we find the greatest exercise of all the gifts of the Holy
Spirit and hear the Lord speaking to us.

Throughout the growth of our experience of worship in
the church, the musicians have taken a strong leading role.
Much of the initial vision and the thrust for worship has
come from those involved in the music ministry. However
those with highly developed musical gifts are not always
called to share those gifts in worship. Often they are so busy
with music in their professional lives as musicians that their
service to God's people is best exercised in a totally different area, and we have found it unfair to put any pressure on
such musicians to contribute regularly in worship. Times
when they have contributed, for example during special

events at Easter, Christmas and so on, have proved to be that much more of a blessing to them and to the congregation because they are rarely used. Our experience has shown us that we should not automatically assume that those who are gifted musicians are also gifted in leading worship.

The fellowship of prayer and practice together was, and still is, the most vital feature of the music groups. Without spiritual and musical harmony between musicians and singers, we are like blunted swords in the Lord's hand; our cutting edge against the kingdom of darkness is ineffectual, and the church suffers. The original grouping of musicians has now widened, and we are finding an increasing number of people called and equipped to join the music ministry. We have found that all our musicians sense the call to what they are doing, virtually to the exclusion of any other regular ministry in the church. They have a vision of where the Lord is taking us.

Renewal is of course much more than just changes in the form of service and the music. To rely on these alone would simply be to put new icing on what could be an old, mouldy cake! This would be counterfeit renewal and deceitful not only to those outside the church but indeed to ourselves. The changes in worship have been part of a wide range of radical changes in the life of the fellowship, and have taken place against a background of such things as preaching, teaching, one-to-one ministry, introductory courses and church membership classes. In these ways we have set out to ground our people in the true understanding of what worship is and how to participate fully in it, as something which is woven into the whole pattern of Christian discipleship. Virtually all the teaching, both in material for others to use and in the actual teaching, has come from our former pastor, Nigel.

Problems in Worship

New forms of worship introduced into the services were a major cause of disquiet among the more traditional members of the fellowship. Voices were raised in the form of letters in the church magazine and at church members' meetings, and allegations of worship becoming 'songs around the campfire' were made. The situation was met by a ground swell of new life within the church. As matters came to a head, there were meetings about the way forward in the music ministry, as a result of which the choir members decided they would disband. Essentially what happened was that the old structure gave under intense pressure from the new growth within the church and the new life of the Holy Spirit in people's lives.

One of the main causes of the friction seemed to be a genuine lack of understanding of the new forms of songs in worship, and this aspect of our music produced most contention. Questions such as 'Why did we sing things through twice?' or 'Why such simple words and simple music?' were posed, and admittedly in the early days our songs may have lacked theological depth and musical quality in comparison to the hymns. Still the songs were a contemporary tool for the expression of the worship of our hearts, and the popular nature of the songs made them understandable, memorable and easy to use. The simplicity, coupled with the growing use of the overhead projector, enabled people to be free to worship without worrying about books in their hands.

One of the most contentious issues was the removal of pews to accommodate the new musicians—removal of pews was almost sacrilegious to many. Certainly some of the objections had validity, but the old ways were under pressure, and some members could not or would not move.

A stronger, vibrant congregation was emerging, and nineteenth-century patterns of worship would have stifled twentieth-century hearts. Perhaps those members who did not really understand what was going on did not express their concerns strongly enough, or perhaps we ourselves did not listen enough.

A number of members left the church, but the church as a body—as Ansdell Baptist Church—stayed firmly together. We tried wherever possible to maintain the bond of peace. We apologised not for our convictions but for our wrong attitudes. When people decided to leave, we tried to part company with grace and blessing, and this was reciprocated in nearly every case. It is possible that confrontation arose out of frustration with the old ways, and perhaps if we had taken a step backwards to look at the situation, confrontation could have been avoided. But for almost everyone, even in the older age range, the movement of the Holy Spirit was clear; the fresh air was blowing through the church, and some of our older members who had prayed for revival within it rejoiced to see this new life when change finally began. The people of the church now believed that as a many-membered body, we all had a part to play in worship—in fact, the lid was off! What did this mean for us? There was no longer a choir; we were left to find other church members' skills on the organ, and we coped! A piano was purchased, and the music group comprising three girl singers, two male guitarists/vocalists, bass and piano came to the fore.

The Leadership of Ansdell

A word here about the position of the leading pastor or

minister. His role is difficult, yet crucial. If he is not in favour of allowing the congregation freedom to be led by the Holy Spirit, or finds this threatening to his own position, he can be the greatest block to change, since ultimately he is in charge of the weekly worship of the church. If however he is in favour of allowing such freedom, he stands in the difficult position of needing to keep good order and be a pioneer, and yet at the same time to make room for the congregation to mature and develop in the skills of participation. This participation accords of course with Baptist theology, where the church meeting *together* discerns the mind of Christ. The reality however may be that he finds himself caught between flak from those who do not wish to move so quickly, or to move at all, and criticism from others who do not feel that things are moving nearly as fast as they should be! In this unenviable position—which he occupied for the last thirteen years—Pastor Nigel Wright managed with the wisdom and help of the Lord to steer the Church with the help of elders and deacons through all the changes. He placed a high priority on keeping our church family substantially whole. Now he has left us with a strong leadership structure which is well practised in the gift of leading in worship, and our congregation has confidence in that leadership. There has been tremendous team work and mutual trust between musicians, worship leaders, the pastor and his elders, without which we would not be where we are now in our worship together. We have desired to respect and honour one another in the Lord, and the role of the pastor in holding the helm has been vital. At times when people want to move too quickly ahead, the pastor is the one to urge patience and restraint under the guidance of the Holy Spirit for the good of all the people.

The major forms which we use in worship have been

music, the spoken word through preaching and prayer, prophetic words of knowledge and other gifts of the Spirit. The strength of the music ministry has largely arisen out of the background of contemporary music within the church, and although we use drama and dance at major events or family services, drama and dance worship forms are generally used as message carriers in evangelism. Music has been found to be the main ministry to and from the people, encouraging and allowing them to express worship—no doubt because people can identify so closely with music. It is one of the most powerful gifts to the church as our whole being is touched when we sing or are ministered to in song.

Our leadership structures for the service now come out of a worship team which meets every week, where ideas are shared and plans made. A service leader is responsible for the over-all presentation and direction of the service; a worship leader who is always a musician is in control of the group of musicians; and the preacher is the third member of the team. The service leading and worship leading roles can combine in one person, but we are increasingly finding the three-fold grouping to be of great strength as each supports the other. We find that the service leader shares in creating the security and structure of the services and in giving it direction. He is usually an elder, although others are regularly used.

In planning, those responsible for the service choose the songs we are to use. The direction of the service is planned generally along a theme which reflects a sense of what God's particular concern for us is at the present time, or which may tie in closely with the message to be preached. Although this pattern is generally followed, the service is open to change under the direct inspiration of the Holy Spirit through any one of the three leading. Further modification may come from the people themselves by a song, a prayer, a prophecy or a simple word spoken out; in this case the word is first tested by those leading, and the word is taken up and followed through. Mutual support is perhaps the best way to summarise the interaction in meetings and services.

Worship at Ansdell

The service usually starts with a call to worship in the form of a Scripture reading or theme explained followed by a prayer asking the Lord for his presence and blessing upon his people gathered. There then generally follows a time of praise and worship along the theme the service leader senses is God's concern for us, with the aim of focussing people's attention in worship and praise to God. We have found a useful method is that of linking songs together, either rehearsing the links beforehand (particularly where there is a change of key from one song to another) or staying in the same key and continuing with a song on the same theme.

Over the years we have gathered a repertoire of more than 250 songs, so that our choice of theme and style is quite wide. We prefer a flow of songs with as little interruption as possible, which we believe leads to unnecessary stops and starts and introductions such as 'now let's sing...' We believe the Lord speaks to the people through what those songs express. If used rightly by the people they take the people individually and corporately into God's presence. Of course at times encouragement along the way is appropriate, but we find this to be rare indeed. We often find that there is a crucial song during these times which actually unlocks the worship in people's hearts. Much of the gift of leading the people is in recognising and pursuing that song and the sense which the Lord wants to convey through it.

A generally adopted pattern follows the Biblical idea of 'entering His gates with thanksgiving' with strong, lively songs of joy and affirmation of God's purposes for us: declaring his praise, his worth, his glory. We can dance, clap and shout joyfully to the Lord (all Scriptural injunctions) giving pleasure to our Father and enjoying ourselves with him in his 'courts'. Entering those courts and moving closer to him along the model of the Old Testament temple, we begin to sense his glory, his beauty, his holiness. Now our praise and joy turn to quiet awe, wonder, worship and adoration. Equally the gathering might start with quieter, more reflective songs, setting our hearts and minds in the Lord's direction and then moving off from that point into stronger praise. There is often a 'flavour' to the gathering which can be different every time we meet, but which can usually be perceived—often before the service in times of prayer, or very quickly after the start. The responsibility falls upon both the service and worship leaders to prepare the service prayerfully but always be ready to hear the Lord and change their plans as he directs.

The reflective approach to the Lord follows a pattern of moving into God's presence with the use of gentle songs, as we want to give and receive from him; we find that the Holy Spirit usually directs clearly from that point. Then we move into other songs and forms of participation as he leads. We usually find that there is a natural break in the worship where songs subside and when people are encouraged to pray and contribute spontaneously. This time in the service comes to an end as the service leader draws into a closing prayer, perhaps crystallising our thoughts and putting us to action. The administrative parts of the services follow:

notices, taking the offering, etc. These, we find, form a natural breather for people; we have found that we must be aware of and respect people's limits of concentration.

More often than not we then enter into another time of worship, settling into his presence and sensing the intimacy of our relationship with him as Father. Often what the Lord is saying to us as a church may come through strongly in the prophetic word and shared Scripture, vision or prayer. We find that there are seasons in the life of the church when he speaks on specific issues such as repentance, proclamation, holiness, or healing. It is in these quieter and more intimate times when we use more lyrical songs, that we find the more overt gifts of the Spirit are used.

In more recent times, probably for the last two or three years, we have experienced a growth in the use of 'singing in the Spirit'. This we can generally define as singing out corporately our individual worship to God in improvised song, either in English or in the spiritual language of tongues. We find when we use this gift that it unlocks deeper worship again both for the individual and for the body; it also gives God a greater space to work, particularly in the areas of intercession and personal commitment. Singing in the Spirit does not have to be solely in the quieter more intimate times, of course, and it can be used in a proclamatory, affirmatory manner also.

Following on from this second time of worship, whoever is teaching will start his sermon at an appropriate time. Teaching is more often than not on a theme that the pastor is preaching a series on, after which there may be a further opportunity to respond in prayer, worship and commitment.

One encouragement to the church for quite a while was ministry for healing or other forms of prayer when they were appropriate, usually after the evening service. During these times worship would continue as people came forward to be prayed for. We also now have services where people are specifically encouraged to come and pray for others and be prayed for themselves. Words of knowledge often come in these times to direct and encourage those involved. Communion is shared morning or evening, two or three times a month, and we now receive the wine from six or eight cups, with one loaf, and no longer use the more traditional Baptist method of separate small glasses and small individual pieces of bread. Again a small thing which we have found to be of a blessing to us as it expresses more readily the truths of communion together.

We have found for the sake of simplicity two distinct levels of worship. There is first of all praise to God, ascribing the honour and glory to his name which is his due, but then there is the sharing of intimate moments with our Father, abiding in his presence and simply enjoying him.

The Past and Future of Ansdell

We have found that the opening up of worship to the movement of the Holy Spirit has given us the life which the Holy Spirit can bring. Despite the negative attitudes that have sometimes surfaced we experience the living God walking among his people, touching and changing us—it is exciting and awe-inspiring. We can never 'box up' the Lord; he may work in ways which we would not choose. An example of this came during the 'Vineyard' visit of John Wimber when the manifestation of God's power was so evident that a number of people simply could not physically stand in his presence and fell to the ground. There was again much heart-searching and genuine questioning from the people. What was this? Is it God's work? What does the Bible say— all genuine questions that had to be worked through. Again, however, the questioning has promoted growth and a deeper understanding of God.

The tempo of growth has been affected so much that our ordinary worship services act as an evangelistic outreach because when an unbeliever comes in he knows that there is something going on. One comment recently was 'Even if I don't believe, it's obvious that you do. I will be back.' We find that whenever God is praised and worshipped he is there in the midst. It is for him to speak to the people; and he does! People are drawn to this form of worship. It has been a major factor in the church's growth so that we have now divided into three fellowships in Blackpool, Lytham and in an outlying village of Freckleton. We meet as a total congregation at celebrations monthly in the evening, and these are strategic times in the church's life. We are finding that the central church at Ansdell is filling up again.

As we look back, it is probably true to say that we would change nothing of what we have done. Perhaps we would change the *way* we have done things. Perhaps we could have created more security in changing times, and perhaps if we had discerned the body better, the resistance encountered would not have been so strong, and we might have been more gracious. Having said this, in any move of God one is bound to hit opposition and must calculate upon its coming. If asked to sum up what we have learned in all this, it could be 'move with purpose but with patience'.

But what about future developments? The worship ministry of the church is now starting to reach out. One of the longest-standing groups, Habitation, has made a tape through Ears and Eyes Production Company, which is based in Leeds. The tape 'You Lift up My Heart' has sold reasonably with good reviews in the Christian media.

Our major songwriter, Bob Fraser, has had a number of songs featured on the Ears and Eyes recordings for 'Song of Renewal' and 'True Worship'. We have always aimed to take what the Lord has given us to other fellowships, teaching and sharing not just in music any more, but using the whole range of ministry that has developed within the church—in the sharing of gifts and also teaching. Nigel Wright was called upon in a number of situations where people from church supported him. Teams are sent out with the aim of working to promote renewal. Also, through close relationship with other ministers, priests and pastors, we are seeing a growth in recent days of fellowship between brothers and sisters in other denominations. We hold meetings with the Church of England, Full Gospel and Catholic churches from Lancaster, Fleetwood, Fulwood, and Preston respectively; and at our last gathering in an hotel in Blackpool there were over 550 people present. We have found true unity in the Holy Spirit on the common ground of worshipping and learning together.

For ourselves we recognise that we have only just begun. Our times together can be so much deeper with the Lord. They can be so much richer and more wholesome as our worship becomes more varied, releasing more and more creativity, touching more and more needs, and encouraging more and more people.

We know we are still standing on the edge of what the Lord has for us and we see in part only the depths to which he can take us. It is as if we were on the borders of the Promised Land. We can smell the grass and the fruit on the wind inviting and enticing us. Like C S Lewis's characters Polly and Digory at the dawning of Aslan's creation of

Narnia in *The Magician's Nephew*, we smell the freshness of a new world and wait with eager expectation and excitement. We know that we must strengthen what we already have and our current thoughts are towards consolidation and moving on from there. Very much like Joshua we are told to be 'strong and of good courage' (Joshua 1:9).

Chapter 5

New Life Christian Fellowship Lincoln

Stuart Bell and John Shelbourne

What happens when an Assemblies of God fellowship merges with an unaffiliated charismatic group? This chapter answers that question, showing how Evangel Church and Lincoln Free Church joined together in 1983 to produce New Life Christian Fellowship—a group committed to developing its own expression of worship through cells, congregation, and celebrations. From the centre of Lincoln it now reaches out to a wider area that extends from the Humber to the Wash.

Authors John Shelbourne and Stuart Bell, both full-time ministers, describe their emphasis on evangelism, friendship among members of the leadership (seven in all), and congregational participation. They write honestly about tensions within the church, and about their concern that Christ indeed be present in their worship.

John and Stuart are both married and both enjoy gardening (or in John's case—watching his wife gardening). Stuart worked for 11 years with the evangelistic team the Advocates, and John did two years' mission work in Zaïre before both settled down to their ministry in Lincoln.

So this is the building where the newly formed, vibrant, charismatic fellowship is going to meet?

A majestic edifice right in the centre of the city. An

impressive spire towering above most of the surrounding
buildings. Stained glass windows losing some of their
beauty by the grime picked up over the years. Inside pews
to seat approximately 1,000, rigid and immovable in their
formation. A magnificently carved pulpit 'high and lifted
up', behind it a marvellous and gigantic pipe organ, accompanied by seating for one lonely organist.

How would a congregation which enjoys lots of movement and expression enjoy worship in such surroundings?
This was the beginning of an exciting and painful experience.

City

Lincoln is a city of about 75,000 people. Throughout its history it has been influenced by the Romans, Danes and Nor-
mans. The latter built a castle and cathedral, which still
overshadow the city after 900 years. It was in this city that
New Life Christian Fellowship was born in 1983, and we believe it will leave its mark and influence. Each week about
600 people belonging to this fellowship meet in various set-
tings to worship the Lord.

An Environment of Worship

Over 40 years ago a nucleus of dedicated Christians met together in a small rented room in Lincoln. The message that
they proclaimed was new, relevant and radical at the time.
It re-emphasised the need to be open to the power and
anointing of the Holy Spirit. Though still few in number this
group of believers moved into an old Methodist church in

the south of the city and became a force for the kingdom of God in the immediate area. Many others began to learn from their experience, and often people from the traditional churches visited with a view to seeing what was the secret of their growing success. Thus this Assemblies of God church developed, eventually moving into large premises in the centre of the city. John Shelbourne, who led this work, was later joined by John Phillips, who took on the responsibility for Bible teaching. Together they began to build the fellowship and saw it grow. The fellowship became known as Evangel Church.

Meanwhile during the 1970's a charismatic group developed in the city. Twenty or thirty Methodists were baptised in the Holy Spirit and began to meet together on Thursday evenings. Among these were four young men known as 'the Advocates', who were involved in evangelism with British Youth for Christ. During a time of outreach in the city a number of young people became Christians. They found it difficult to fit into the church structures, and a small group began to meet—firstly in the church and later in the house of Stuart Bell—one of the Advocates. In 1976 this small nucleus became known as Lincoln Free Church. After humble beginnings in a hired hall, the fellowship grew in numbers and by seven years later consisted of around 120 committed people. This number was predominately made up of new converts, the majority under the age of 35.

During this time Lincoln Free Church developed house groups; it became noticeable that the way these were moving was similar to that of Evangel Church, and that the visions and goals for the city and area were very similar for both groups. As people passed one another to go to house groups, it became evident that God was speaking to us about unity in his body. Stuart Bell, John Shelbourne and John Phillips met together in 1983 to discuss the possibilities of joining forces, recognising that God had not come to take sides but had, in a real sense, come to take over. The seeds of unity were set in their hearts, and they then pursued the difficult task of bringing both congregations together under the name of New Life Christian Fellowship.

The coming together was obviously a time of difficulty and of shaking up. Ministries joined together to be part of a team consisting of John Phillips, Stuart Bell and John Shelbourne. Chris Bowater took on responsibilities as musical director, Roger Keel dealt with the administrative side of things; and others handled office functions.

New Life Christian Fellowship is therefore an interesting mix of background and tradition and is now looking to develop its own colouring in the expression of worship. The Pentecostal and charismatic roots have made the blend of worship interesting and original. At times it is also amusing. There was one occasion when, with a sense of community and fellowship we decided to dig and build our own baptistry. It looked quite a good job through the eyes of Christian love.

Whilst baptising a good number of candidates, we realised that we were losing about an inch of water per candidate. This called for shorter testimonies and quicker action!

Expressions of Worship

Various kinds of meetings within New Life Christian Fellowship have been designed to meet differing needs among the people. The type of worship will therefore vary according to the aim and purpose of each meeting. There are three kinds of meetings within the structure of the fellowship as far as the city worship is concerned.

Cell

This is the smallest meeting within the fellowship and takes the form of house groups that are spread throughout the city with people being drawn together mainly on a geographical basis. Worship within this cell is usually informal and often takes the form of singing led by a single guitarist. There is opportunity for sharing and prayer. The purpose of this group is mainly caring and pastoral oversight. Worship is spontaneous with as much praise and participation as possible; prayer times are open and are encouraged by the house group leader.

Congregation

This is the gathering together of four or five house groups within a locality, roughly between 50 and 120 people. The aim of the congregation is to encourage as much participation from the 'body' as is possible. The scriptural context for this can be seen in I Corinthians 14:26: 'What then shall we say, brothers? When you come together, everyone has a hymn, or a word of instruction, a revelation, a tongue or an interpretation. All of these must be done for the strengthening of the Church.'

The format is simple, and worship normally consists of people singing together, rejoicing, praying and sharing testimony. The burden of the meeting is to develop people individually and to help them to move together under the Holy Spirit as a body of people. The size of this gathering allows for a family atmosphere. It is also an ideal size for the congregation leader to be able to recognise people who may have gifts in speaking, sharing or leadership. Within the church we have a large number of musicians, and the congregations allow for many of these to be involved.

Worship is of a spontaneous nature, singing, clapping, dancing, raising of hands and sharing in tongues, interpretations, and prophecy. The congregation is also flexible enough to be able to have evenings when musicians can share, when groups of actors bring drama, or when the children are given opportunity to participate. Evangelism and growth are also vital ingredients. There has been some resistance in the fellowship to new forms of worship, and we have been aware that there is a great need to teach continually that the congregation is not enclosed by a building but is *people*.

Celebration

This is the time when the whole fellowship gathers together. The main ingredients of this gathering are periods of worship with an atmosphere of victory and praise, fellowship, the breaking of bread and teaching. This meeting is generally led from the front with the leader and musicians usually having a framework set out beforehand. Sometimes this is quite rigid, though leader and musicians alike seek to be open to the guidance of the Holy Spirit. The emphasis is worshipping God together as a body of people, and worship is seen as a journey into the presence of God.

The musicians play an active role in preparing the way for God to move among his people and during celebration scriptural expressions of worship are encouraged. We use as our basis of celebration some of the verses listed here:

The use of instruments 'Praise him with the sounding of the trumpet: praise him with the harp and lyre' (Ps 150:3).

The use of voices 'My mouth will speak in praise of the Lord. Let every creature praise his holy name for ever and ever' (Ps 145:21).

The raising of hands 'I want men everywhere to lift up holy hands in prayer, without anger or disputing' (I Tim 2:8).

The clapping of hands 'Clap your hands, all you nations: shout to God with cries of joy' (Ps 47:1).

Dancing 'Let them praise his name with dancing and make music to him with tambourine and harp' (Ps 149:3).

Due to our traditions and upbringing we are still a little weak on certain other scriptural expressions such as *bowing*—Psalm 135:1-2, *kneeling*—Ezra 9:5, and *lying down*—Revelation 4:9-10.

Gifts of the Spirit are used within the context of the celebration, though normally the elders would be in a position to weigh any words of prophecy that are to be brought in order that the service can run without confusion. The music for this service is of the highest quality possible and singing in languages given by the Spirit is often a part of the service. The main teaching follows the worship and, where possible, every effort is made for the theme of the meeting to be followed in the worship and the teaching. When possible the worship is designed to dovetail with the teaching for the day.

From Humber to the Wash

The vision of New Life Christian Fellowship is now beginning to extend beyond the city boundaries and surrounding villages into the area between the Humber and the Wash. In 1982 the vision was born in Lincoln Free Church when the Lincolnshire Showground was hired for a weekend of celebration know as 'Grapevine Celebration'. The first celebration drew about 1,000 people. Now the celebration , which is an annual event, is attracting about 3,500 throughout the weekend. The worship at each Grapevine Celebration takes place within the atmosphere of festival and joy. It is a whole-hearted celebration with praise, clapping and dancing, an abundance of music and a sense of victory throughout the camp.

The scriptural picture that fits this kind of gathering is seen in certain Old Testament celebrations. Under the rule of King David the people brought the Ark of the Covenant into the City of David with great rejoicing. 'He and the entire house of Israel brought up the ark of the Lord with shouts and the sound of trumpets' (II Sam 6:15). A similar time of rejoicing can be found in the days of Nehemiah when against all the odds the walls of Jerusalem were rebuilt. 'And on that day they offered great sacrifices, rejoicing because God had given them great joy. The woman and children also rejoiced. The sound of rejoicing in Jerusalem could be heard far away' (Neh 12:43).

Thoughts of open-air ministry with periods of praise and worship are being explored for the future. The visit of Terry Law to the church in 1985 brought new concepts of worship, recognising that as Christians we are in conflict with evil spiritual powers.

It is time for believers to gain a proper understanding of their authority and the full extent of spiritual warfare raging around them. It is time to more effectively and victoriously enter the battle and begin pulling down the enemy's strongholds. Healing and deliverance—the pulling down of strongholds—will come through praise and worship.[1]

This developing vision has taken on real substance as a group of men now relate and share together with a view of strategic evangelism and church planting programmes. Bob Lenton from Horncastle and Dave Kitchen from Grimsby have joined the local men in this particular vision. Worship, of course, is a key factor, and there is a new awareness of the relationship between worship and praise and evangelism.

Evangelism and Worship

At the present time we have a great concern for evangelism and church planting; we feel that the key to some of these things is in the realm of worship. In the future New Life Christian Fellowship aims to reach out into four areas of the city. The evangelism approach will not be along the usual lines. Four sports centres have been booked for the outreaches, and Chris Bowater brought the idea of 'The Good News Time Machine'. This will be a multi-media presentation which aims to include all members of the fellowship in some way or other. People have been challenged to be involved in as many as forty different ways: from stewarding and baking to hairdressing and puppet-making. All kinds of activities are to be included: from the more traditional such as drama, dance, music and praise, to the more unusual such as BMX cycling and sports activities. The aim therefore is to present in many forms the concept that to worship God involves the whole of our lives laid down for the Lord. Worship is always productive, bringing glory to God and changing the lives of his people.

Relationships between Leaders and Musicians

In the celebration style and development of worship, gone are the days when the programme was solely between the minister and the organist, who hoped he would still be able to see the minister through his mirror, though mainly from behind a curtain. What a marvellous setting for relationships!

A totally different scene reveals itself today. Probably anything up to a dozen musicians plus half a dozen lead singers, interwoven with wires, plugs and monitors; microphones and amplifiers standing like guards on duty, defying the uninitiated to move them. A far cry from Wesley and Whitefield, though the same Spirit is at work! This style of worship is filling the largest halls throughout the country. Charismatic worshippers have made these places echo with vibrant worship. Every known instrument is blown or played for the glory of God—and on one occasion we visited a fellowship where worship was even led by someone playing a saw! No longer do new converts have to hide their instruments or put them away in the loft, just having the occasional glance when they think about the good old days. As well as dedicating their lives to the Lord they are able to dedicate musical instruments and get involved in worship to the glory of God. With all this taking place how do things stay in control and come under the heading of 'decently and in order'? We have found the answer in three essential components to our worship.

Friendship

It is obvious that in a large and growing fellowship one cannot have a deep relationship with all the musicians in the church, but one can pray and understand this special breed of folk. What makes them tick? What are they really trying to express through and with their varied instruments? In a growing church with many instrumentalists there must be a chief musician or music director. It is absolutely necessary for the minister to have a good friendship with such a person. It is impossible to hope to lead worship together and still be almost strangers with each other.

Worship is to do with unity, harmony, a thing of the Spirit. It cannot be turned on but can only flow from an immediate experience. One therefore needs to work on building up such a friendship: to show interest in each other's family, dreams and ambitions, having times together outside a church setting. As this friendship develops, minister and musician become aware of each other's weaknesses and strengths. They begin to know each other when their guards are down—the good and bad points. True friendship wants to see success in its friends; to work to the end that they may find fulfilment and be a blessing in the fellowship. And this is what happens, we have found, when minister and musician become friends.

Frankness

We are told that God is looking for worshippers to worship him in Spirit and in Truth (reality). This is an essential ingredient in worship. There can be no pretence in true worship. But there are times when frankness can be costly. It may seem easier at times to sweep things under the carpet, pretending that some mannerism isn't really annoying us, and if we ignore it, it will go away. Experience teaches us, however, that things don't go away; they just increase and reappear at a most inconvenient time. On the basis of true friendship, we can afford to confront each other frankly, remembering that we want each other to succeed. This honesty will enable us to 'flow' together as we lead the congregation in worship.

Flowing

It is of great importance that leaders and musicians should develop a close rapport together if they are going to lift the congregation in worship. Uncertainty in either leaders or musicians will hinder the congregation. If those leading are not sure where they are going, what hope is there for those who are supposed to be following? Worship interrupted by too many contributions at the wrong times (however spiritual they may seem) can be completely marred.

What, then, are some of the things that will help leaders and musicians flow together? In New Life Christian Fellowship whoever is leading the worship meets with the chief musician and discusses with him or her what direction they will be taking in worship and what they are hoping to accomplish. Some people may object to discussing beforehand. They feel this can take the spontaneity out of it. They say 'Why don't you just let it happen?' We have tried that method and prefer discussion. Although thoughts are aired together before worship, there is still enough flexibility if the Holy Spirit has other ideas.

Also, in discussing worship, we may start with songs of

thanksgiving, then praise flowing into heartfelt worship of God for who he is. It is necessary to know the direction together. It doesn't help at all if one is feeling in a marching, military type of mood and the other very reflective. It is not sufficient to express our own feelings but ask 'What is the Spirit saying to the church?'

As the leader cannot keep his eye on all the musicians, it is important that arrangements are made for their direction. That is where the chief musician comes in. There are times when all the instrumentalists are involved in victorious mood; occasions also when the instrumentalists cease to accompany the worship, and one just hears the hundreds of voices joined together; or the occasion when only a few of the musicians minister; or times when perhaps just a single instrument will take the lead in worship. It has been known for the drummer to give a 'victory roll'—or serve notice to the Enemy that the church is in war against him. Unless the person leading the worship is familiar with the musicians and some of these expressions, he is going to be left standing like a spare part.

Sometimes the worship is led by the person in the pulpit, other times by the chief musicians. The problems arise when one is not certain who is taking the lead. This also affects the congregation, who do not know where to look for direction. Worship then almost looks like a tennis match, all eyes going from one to another. If we are going to flow together, then we must be familiar with each other. Experience has taught both the leaders and chief musicians that one must be sure who is in charge at any particular time. We cannot emphasise how important it is for our fellowship to 'flow' together.

What of the Future?

A W Tozer describes worship as the missing jewel of the Church. We are living in times when that jewel is being re-discovered and its multi-faceted sides polished. Yes, some mistakes may have been made; some extravagances may have taken place, but many marvellous things are happening in this dimension. We feel sure that the twentieth-century Church will once again move in the power of first-century worship and go on to pioneer depth and quality of worship not hitherto known to any age of the Church.

You may ask what we are looking for in the future as a church. At least four elements will characterise our worship.

Presence of Christ

We know that Jesus is omnipresent, but our desire is to see that presence made manifest in all we do. That does not mean we are always in deadly earnest; on the contrary, as worship has become more exuberant, the instrumentalists have become more enthusiastic. On one occasion, the lid of the grand piano parted company with the rest of the instrument. And on another, one instrumentalist played so enthusiastically that he showed a clean pair of heels as he disappeared off the edge of the platform! So we enjoy our worship together!

We are discovering many new techniques—forming many new liturgies, excelling in our music, and many new worship songs are blessing the church. But what advantage are all these things if they do not bring a consciousness of the presence of Jesus? Our praise and worship may be amongst the most enthusiastic. We may have raised its fervour by several decibels, but if it does not bring a sense of Christ's presence, it is in vain. We don't want people taken up with our style of worship, or the lovely music, or the raising of the hands or even our dancing before the Lord. If all these things do not draw people to Jesus, we have missed the mark. No one will leave a gathering dissatisfied if they have sensed his presence to heal, or comfort, reassure. His very presence brings us to repentance.

Power of Christ

Another deep longing in our hearts is that Christ may also manifest his power as we worship him. As the hymn says:

> *Jesus, stand amongst us*
> *In your risen power—*

When we look around the Church of Jesus Christ, we see a powerless Church. There are many people spiritually and physically sick, and the Church seems almost impotent against evil. Many seem to be imprisoned by old thought-patterns, and it seems almost impossible to change their way of thinking. So it is in our conflict with Satan. How easily we look for natural explanations for spiritual problems and end up wrestling with 'flesh and blood' when in fact our warfare is against principalities and powers, against spiritual wickedness in high places. What we long to see, through the worship in our church, are the strongholds of Satan pulled down and the sick healed. The power of Christ can indeed be revealed through worship!

Prophetic Worship

There is much debate these days whether we use hymn books or overhead projectors. Should we sing old-fashioned hymns or contemporary songs? This silly argument is often used to justify our own cherished position. We need hymns, however old, that are based on doctrinal truth—truth that does not change with the centuries. (Thank God for some of the ancient hymn writers.)

What a tragedy, though, when we can only sing of someone else's experience one hundred or more years ago. How sad when we can only sing of a revival that happened somewhere in history—when we have to borrow someone else's experience to sing of God's provision or deliverance. If we are a relevant church we must have an up-to-date experience. We must proclaim what God is doing today in today's idiom. He is not just yesterday's God. He is the same today and has things to say today. He can show us things today about tomorrow's world and help us to live in the light of that revelation.

If God is speaking about unity, let our lifestyle and worship proclaim this truth. If God is speaking about signs and wonders, let us make room in our worship for these things to take place. If God is speaking about caring in the Church, or a social concern for things outside the Church, let our worship and involvement be a visual aid. Let us have ears to hear what the Spirit is saying to the churches. Having received and understood the mind of Christ, let us proclaim it in our worship and practise it in our commitment. Having heard the voice of the Spirit, let us live it. Let us walk in the light. We do not want to be prisoners of history, but children of a living, dynamic God who transcends history.

Participating Congregation

We have always encouraged congregational participation, but we long to see this greatly extended: to see expressions that bring a spirit of conviction and not confusion, so that without embarrassment the church lifts up its voice together in united prayer, praise and worship; to see people freed from the prison-like confines of the pews and to feel a new sense of mobility and flexibility; not to feel that one has to be regimented during the worship and only allowed freedom after the final AMEN.

God's message to Pharaoh was 'Let my people go.' Perhaps we have done what Pharaoh couldn't do, that is, made prisoners out of God's people. But we want them to make contact with each other—a closeness, a true spirit of fellowship. We want them to have opportunity to follow the injunction of James, who said, 'Pray one for another that you might be healed' (made whole, enjoy fulfilment). We would love to see the participation of believers grow. As the worship grows, Christian concern flows from the people into the community, into areas of hurt—in other words, our lives (and thus others') are completely remade. We cannot worship in isolation; once we participate in worship we are *involved*.

For our coming together is for God's glory. We come to meet with him, to worship him, to hear his voice. If this takes place, no one will go home disappointed. Fear and self-consciousness in worship rob us of freedom of expression in that worship. God wants us to do far more in his Church than we allow him to do. It is my desire to see this kind of worship finding its birth in the entire church. That truly will establish his glory among us and out of that his Kingdom will grow in Lincoln.

Do we hear you say, 'If you go for these things, and allow such freedom, think of all that could go wrong'?

We would not want to take the risk element out of our Christian life. We need to adventure into worship.

THINK OF ALL THE THINGS THAT COULD GO RIGHT!

Note

1 Terry Law, *The Power of Praise and Worship* (Victory House: Tulsa, 1985), p 34.

Chapter 6

Chapel St Methodist Church Penzance, Cornwall

John Horner

Chapel St Methodist Church is in the traditional and conservative town of Penzance (population 15,000). The original congregation was formed in the mid 1700's, and John Wesley himself preached to it several times. Today it is housed in what the author describes as 'a bastion of respectability'— one of the oldest, largest and most splendid chapels of British Methodism. But numbers declined, and by the 1970's there was talk of closure.

Change came in 1984 when a core of members who had been praying for renewal saw prayers answered as new Bible study groups and prayer fellowships began to form. Fallow ground was broken up, and people who had found the worship 'dull and irrelevant' became involved in an innovative evening service which allowed for congregation participation, lay leadership and free-flowing praise—and which grew in numbers beyond all expectation.

John Horner has a Master of Arts degree in Sociology and a Bachelor of Divinity degree. He is married with two sons and a daughter and spends his spare time writing, sketching, listening to classical music and exploring off-the-map England.

A Bastion of Tradition and Respectability

The Chapel St Methodist Chapel, Penzance, looks like a bastion of tradition and respectability. It is—or was. The church as a fellowship dates back to the days of John Wesley himself. It is likely that he founded it. It is certain that he preached to it. And shortly after Wesley's last visit to Penzance in 1789, Maria Branwell—mother of the Brontë sisters and a Wesleyan Methodist—became a member of the church before she left Cornwall for Yorkshire, Patrick Brontë and the Church of England.

The present chapel was built not long after England first learned of the victory of Trafalgar from an announcement made in the Penzance public assembly rooms a few doors away from the Chapel St chapel. Today the building stands four square and forbidding behind its impressive cast-iron railings. The embellishment of an Italianate portico added in the 1860's softens somewhat the grim, grey granite façade.

But inside things are different. Here there is lightness and brightness. The large galleried interior is decorated in white and pale blue and 23 stained glass windows add rich and varied colour. The solid mahogany 'wine-glass' pulpit with its elegant curving stairs and balustrades is a magnificent feature. A visiting American recently offered to give us several thousand dollars if we would let him take it back to the States!

But a church cannot live on tradition, even if it does go back to John Wesley; or on respectability, even if it has included half the town mayors in its membership; or on the beauty of its interior, even if it is of an outstanding quality. By 1980, in a building designed to seat 1200, the morning congregation had dropped to about 80 and the evening to 18. There was even talk of closing the chapel.

Today we see 200 at our morning service and 120 at the second of our evening services. (For reasons which will be explained later, we have two evening services.) Our three services vary considerably in the type of worship they offer. The range spreads from the full liturgical order of morning worship with communion, as prescribed in the official Methodist Service Book, to spontaneous prayer, praise and prophecy. The musical content can vary from an anthem by Palestrina to chorus singing led by an enthusiastic music group and helped on its way by much congregational hand clapping and the rattle of the occasional tambourine. Happily, the white-collar worshippers are still with us, but the chances are that they will be sitting next to someone in T-shirt and jeans, or even shorts.

Explaining the Growth

How did this change and growth take place? We began where Hosea told the people of his day to begin—by breaking up our fallow ground (Hosea 10:12 AV). Fallow ground is not unproductive ground; it is unproducing ground. There was good ground at Chapel St; it just wasn't producing. There were some lovely, spiritual, committed people who had toiled and dreamed and ached and prayed for years. They were not seeing much for their labours in 1980, but without them the harvest of these days could not have been reaped.

The fallow ground was broken up by persistent, expectant, believing prayer and by the study of, and obedience to, the Word of God. Not that the people had not been praying previously. They had; but on their own. In 1980 we started praying and studying the Bible together. A weekly Friday night prayer meeting and Bible study fellowship was established and given priority in the church's diary. Nothing else was allowed to take place at the same time as this meeting, and the minister never accepted invitations to go to other churches on Friday evenings.

And so about fifteen people began to meet regularly together for prayer and Bible study with the purpose of discovering what the Spirit was saying to our church. Needless to say, we did not at once receive the power or blessings of effective prayer. We found it easier to pray for people's bodily and physical needs than for the spiritual needs of individuals or of the church as a whole. But we kept at it, and God rewarded us, though it was four years or more before it became evident in the church as a whole that God was blessing us.

Hosea also told his people that a time of harrowing would need to follow the ploughing. 'Jacob shall break his clods,' as the Authorised Version vividly puts it (Hosea 10:11). Ploughing produces ridges and furrows as the earth is opened up, and these ridges have to be broken up and softened to help the seed to take root. The ploughing certainly produced ridges at Chapel St, but in this respect Hosea's agricultural metaphor cannot be applied too precisely in our experience. It was the actual sowing of the seed itself— the preaching and teaching of the Word of God—which probably did most to break up the ridges and make the ground productive.

The Catalyst

The catalyst came two and a half years after the present

minister, John Horner, arrived at Chapel St. The youth fellowship, which then totalled seven eleven-to-thirteen-year-olds, was in St Ives enjoying a residential weekend. Their parents had been invited to meet with the minister on the Saturday afternoon to talk about the problems of bringing up children in the Christian faith in a non-Christian environment. Three couples accepted the invitation, and as they talked together it became clear that one of the main problems was the church itself. The parents were frank with us. They themselves were not regular attenders, and they admitted that they did not expect their children to be. Why? Because they did not feel that they related to the worship or it to them. 'The services,' they said, 'are a sort of two-man band devised and presented by the minister and the organist. We have no part in their planning, preparation or follow-up. We are spectators at somebody else's show.'

Many people would react to that by saying that you do not have to have a hand in the planning or presentation of a service to be able to feel a part of the worship. But that was the way this particular group saw things, and we took it from there. John Horner said, 'Suppose we could devise services in which you could be involved in the ways you indicate, would you come? And would you come every week?' 'Yes,' they said. And that 'yes' was to be our turning point at Chapel St.

Having committed ourselves to the creation of a worship service in which all could have a distinct share, we now had two things to do to get it off the ground. First we had to find a time when it could be held. There was no question of adapting the 11 o'clock service. The criticism of the youth fellowship parents expressed the feeling of what was then only a small minority within the church. Most of our regular worshippers liked our services the way they were. They did not want to have a share in the planning, leading or follow-up. For them there was sufficient involvement in singing the hymns, listening to the choir and minister, offering prayer and sitting in quiet contemplation.

We also have a service at 6 o'clock led for the most part by lay preachers. This meets the needs of the small number of people who attend it, and they did not wish to see its format changed. And in any case, John Horner was not free to take part in regular worship at Chapel St at 6 o'clock. As superintendent minister of a Methodist circuit he has a responsibility to lead services in the 12 other churches of the circuit, and this he does in turn at 6 o'clock.

So we settled for 8 o'clock in the evening, a time when John could be back from his services elsewhere in the circuit and therefore free to give the teaching at Chapel St every week. It proved to be a right choice and was particularly popular with families—even with young children—who liked to have a day together on Sundays and could be back home and ready for church by 8 p.m.

The other thing we had to do to get this second evening service off the ground was to set up groups in which we could plan the services together, discuss their theme and format, and appoint people to the various parts they were going to take in sharing the leading of the service. A few other people in addition to the youth fellowship parents showed an interest in 'the 8 o'clock' as it is now called, and two house groups were formed which took it in turn to be responsible for the Sunday service.

The 8 o'clock Takes Shape

Eventually we were ready for the first 8 o'clock. It took place on Easter Sunday 1983 with a congregation of 26. At the time of writing the congregation averages 120 and the number of house groups has grown to 10. These still in turn prepare and share in the leading of the services.

From the outset we agreed that at the 8 o'clock services people were to be free to worship God in whatever way they felt right. Provided, that is, that what they did was a genuine offering to God and not something done to impress or shock others or to draw attention to themselves. The more conventional worshipppers who felt rather threatened or embarrassed by spontaneous and unfamiliar gestures were to honour and respect their brothers and sisters who made them, without feeling obliged to make them themselves. John Horner said something like this, 'If you want to clap your hands during the songs, do so. If it seems right to you in worship to stand and raise your arms, do so. If you want to sit while others stand, or stand while others sit, feel free to do so. And if you want to hide your head behind the safety and security of your songbook, do that. But let's not have half the congregation accusing the other half of being in bondage, and that half regarding the rest as spiritual freaks. Acceptance of one another with all that that means in worship is one of the first lessons we are going to learn of the Lord. And if you can't take it, don't come at 8 o'clock!'

But in making that stand, John was doing more than encouraging people to do whatever *they* felt like doing. He intended, when the time was right, to give teaching on the gifts of the Spirit, and he wanted to prepare an environment in which those gifts could be exercised without fear or restraint whenever God saw fit to give them. That teaching has now been given. God is releasing the gifts of the Holy Spirit amongst us—even the more dramatic gifts—and they are being exercised without causing offence.

Talents, Gifts and Ministries

The release and exercise of spiritual gifts must be seen in the context of a theology of the church. At Chapel St we set ourselves to work out the implications of Paul's teaching about the church as the Body of Christ (I Cor 12:27). Each member of a body has a function, but we felt that we needed to distinguish between natural talents and spiritual gifts, and between gifts and roles (or ministries). We believe that we need to be clear about these distinctions not for academic or legalistic reasons, but for practical and functional purposes. The important thing about a talent or gift is not that it should be correctly identified and labelled, but that it should be used for God's glory. But in order to use it for God's glory, we must be clear about what it is. For instance, a person used by God in an act of healing needs to know whether that was a once only gift of the Spirit graciously given by God to meet that one specific need, or whether it was a sign that that person has been given a healing ministry and can be used repeatedly by God in healing.

On the basis of Scripture, we believe that God has endowed his body with such gifts and ministries as are necessary for its effective functioning. And we believe that every member of the body has at least one gift. Through private conversations and discussions in house groups we have slowly but joyfully discovered our gifts and begun to use them. Broadly speaking, these gifts fall into two categories

—worship talents and gifts and service talents and gifts. Worship talents and gifts include music, drama and graphics and the ability to lead praise and prayer sessions. Of the gifts of the Spirit listed in I Corinthians 12, all have been exercised in worship except, perhaps, the gift of knowledge. Those with a gift of supplication have made themselves known to John Horner who supplies them with prayer concerns and looks upon their ministry of persistent and expectant prayer as being of vital importance in the life of the church. No one except John knows who they are, and they are rarely referred to because we do not want it to be supposed that there is a favoured spiritual elite in the church.

Amongst those whose talents and gifts lie in the sphere of service rather than worship, there are marriage guidance and bereavement counsellors who are a great help in the pastoral work; there are practical folk who paint and decorate and mend furniture and along with our splendid caretaker do countless maintenance and repair jobs around the premises; and there are those who beautify the chapel with artistic floral decorations and those who provide delicious meals for special occasions. Last year a small group constructed a life-size crib scene in the chapel portico, complete with palm trees which are not hard to come by in our part of the world. This was floodlit at night, and people came from all over the town to see it. And there is developing amongst us the gift of hospitality. The house groups (of roughly eight members) have helped to foster this. These do not meet in the same homes each time but go round the homes of as many members as can host a group, and in the three years that the house groups have been in existence they have met in 50 different homes. Other acts of hospitality are constantly taking place. Newcomers to the church are invited to homes for coffee to get to know other church members, and it is no unusual thing for half a dozen members to invite others to their homes for lunch after morning service.

Two other aspects of our worship are worth mentioning. One of them is that we are learning to worship God through our giving of money. Our people have been greatly challenged in this way. More and more are accepting the principle of tithing and are covenanting their giving. Weekly offerings have soared, and our income is now such as has encouraged the church council to advertise for another full-time member of staff. Our giving to missions and to the poor, especially to Christian Aid, has also shown a large increase, and we now give away 20% of our church income.

The other aspect is our involvement in God's ministry of healing. As has been said, we believe that the church is the Body of Christ. Believing that, we also believe that God is willing and able to endow his body in these days with the same qualities with which he endowed the body of Jesus in the days of his flesh. One of these qualities was the power to heal, or rather to be an instrument of God in his ministry of healing. We do not hold healing services as such, but on the principle of James 5:14, we believe that every church member in sickness should be able to call for the elders of the church for a ministry of healing. We make it known that this ministry is available, leaving it to the sick person to take the initative and call for the elders. If the sick person is able to come to the chapel, the anointing with oil and laying on of hands takes place during public worship, with some of the elders coming forward perhaps with close friends of the sick to share in the ministry. If the sick person is unable to come to the chapel, the elders will offer ministry in that person's home. Many have received this ministry, and their testimonies to many forms of healing—of the body, of mind, of memories, of emotions, or relationships—powerfully reveal God at work amongst us.

Difficulties

It would be wrong to give the impression that this change and growth took place without difficulty. 'We don't mind change as long as it doesn't make any difference' is a saying that might well have originated in Cornwall. In 1980 the people of Chapel St knew that something had to be done if the church was not to fade out altogether, but it seemed that they had not thought through the implications of growth and renewal—namely that they inevitably mean change and difference. Somehow the people had managed to hope for an increased congregation without coming to terms with the fact that it would mean having to accept and get to know new, strange, different people. A large congregation was a desirable, but abstract, concept. The main difficulty was not opposition so much as lack of support. Not that the church people were lacking in interest—but that many were willing only to be spectators. Church growth and changes in the church were somewhat anxiously met; many would rather watch than pioneer.

When the 8 o'clock service started and the 6 o'clock folk decided to continue with their service, the minister was instantly accused of having divided the church. For some reason it seemed that a church with two services is not a divided church, but a church with three services is! In spite of the fact that the majority of people attending the 8 o'clock service also attended the 11 o'clock service, John Horner was told that Chapel St was no longer a single church but

two congregations. (Apparently the 6 o'clock had been for-
gotten!) 'Are you one of those peculiar 8 o'clockers?' said
one of our members to another one day.

But with grace, patience and goodwill on all sides we
have worked our way through the growing pains and have
become a strong united body. We are still growing, but the
pains have been reduced to the occasional twinge. Looking
back over the days of upheaval, we realise how much we
have to be thankful for. Very few people left us, and there
was no polarising of a discontented faction around any one
person or cause. Perhaps this was partly due to the fact that
we learned to 'make haste slowly' and accepted Jesus's
principle of growth drawn from the natural world, namely
that it doesn't come from toiling and spinning (i.e. an anxious frenzy of activity) but from its own inner dynamic.

Or perhaps the difficulties were comparatively few because of the nature of the Chapel St people themselves.
True they found it hard to come to terms with the effects of
growth; true they had doubts about the rightness of the 8
o'clock service; true they sat back in calculated caution
when the minister was hoping for a little venturing faith;
but supremely they are a warm, generous, loving, caring
people and these, their strongest characteristics, won
through in the end.

A Typical 8 o'clock

Come with us now to an 8 o'clock service. Why an 8
o'clock? Why not an 11 o'clock? Certainly not because we
consider the 8 o'clock to be the more important service.
Rather do we look upon these two main services as comple-
menting each other. Nor has the 8 o'clock won the support

of all our newcomers. On the contrary, some of those who have come to us with little or no previous church background prefer the traditional 11 o'clock service because there they feel safe. The things that happen there are fairly predictable and happen at a distance. At the 8 o'clock things are unpredictable and can happen uncomfortably close. The person next to you may suddenly lead in prayer, or start the chorus over again, or clap or raise his hands during the singing, or leap up to give an announcement, or come out with the occasional 'Praise the Lord'. All very unnerving if you're not used to this sort of thing and are desperately wondering whether perhaps you are expected to do the same. On the other hand, there are first-timers who much prefer the relaxed atmosphere of the 8 o'clock to the formal predictability of the 11. But we are not going to the 11 o'clock because it is typical of Methodist worship at its best, and if that is what you want, there is probably a sample of it within a few miles of where you live.

Of course, there may be some who, having come with us to our 8 o'clock, may say, 'I don't see why you bothered to write that up. We have that sort of thing every week in our church and have done for years.' To which we reply, 'Praise the Lord! But how did your worship start and how did it evolve?' As we see it, the thing that gives God glory in our instance is not so much what is happening as where it is happening. It is happening in our 1000-seater bastion of tradition and respectability; it is happening in Cornwall, a county noted for its conservative attitudes and where British church growth is among the lowest; and it is happening in a small town where there are three other Methodist churches within a few hundred yards.

We enter the chapel at 7.20 and stand in the spacious carpeted foyer. A few years ago there were pews where we are standing now, but we had the back five rows removed all the way across the chapel and this space under the gallery enclosed. This made a great deal of difference to the fellowship of the church. Before we created the foyer there was only a small vestibule between the outer doors and the worship area. 'Not enough room to be polite,' as one person put it. Certainly there was no room for welcoming people, getting to know them and sharing with one another all the news of the family. In addition to standing room for 200 the foyer has also provided room for a bookstall, a book and tape lending library and a display board.

At this moment some people from the house group on duty are preparing refreshments which will be handed round after the service. In the chapel itself members of the music group are busy setting up mikes and amplifiers and tuning their instruments. Others are quietly moving about putting into position the various bits of furniture we need for the service—a small dais in a central position at the front, on it a lectern and beside it a table for the breaking of bread.

By 7.45 quite a few people have arrived and our 'meet and greet' people are on the job. These are people who have a talent for getting to know new people and for making them feel part of the family. They are on duty every Sunday, though this work is not left solely to them. We frequently stress the fact that it is the privilege and duty of every church member to make others feel at home with us.

Some people have now moved into the chapel, and the music group has started to play and sing a few quiet choruses. When we first started the 8 o'clock, our numbers were small—for the first year they averaged 30—and we insisted that, contrary to the usual Methodist practice— people should occupy pews from the front row backwards rather than from the back row forwards. Now numbers have grown and people sit where they like within certain specified blocks. (We have three aisles and four blocks of pews!)

It is now eight o'clock and time for the service to begin. It is clearly a family service, and visitors are surprised at the number of children present. Nor had we anticipated this when we started the services. But it seems that bedtimes are not what they used to be, and the children seem to enjoy coming.

Worship begins with a time of open praise and prayer. Tonight this is led by one of our members who is gifted for this particular ministry. There is a time of chorus singing, and then the leader invites participation. Several pray short praise and thanksgiving prayers; someone reads a verse or two of Scripture; someone has a prophecy, another a testimony. The praise time ends with a lively song, and the lead given by the music group is supported by a couple of tambourines from somewhere in the congregation.

The mood changes for the breaking of bread, which comes next. Breaking of bread at an evening service? Why not? It was instituted at an evening service! And we have it at every evening service because when we started the 8 o'clock services we agreed to use as a model the four practices of the New Testament church described in Acts 2:42— the apostles' teaching, the fellowship, the breaking of bread, and prayer. And we agreed to have the bread only, not the wine as well. This is not a eucharist, holy communion, sacrament of the Lord's supper (or whatever you choose to call it) but a simple rite affirming the living of Jesus as much as his dying. As the bread sustains us in our physical life, so we celebrate the Lord who sustains us in our whole life. And by sharing the same loaf we affirm our unity with each other, with the whole Church and with Christ himself. But the celebration is of *broken* bread, and we do not forget that Christ's living for us is inseparable from his dying for us.

This thought leads us on to our intercessions as we remember that in Christ's sacrifice 'He took up our infirmities and carried our diseases' (Matt 8:17). By his brokenness we are made whole. The intercessory prayers give another opportunity for sharing by the congregation.

This evening the intercessory prayers are followed by the notices. Trying to find the right spot for the notices has been rather like trying to deal with awkward children. We've got them and we love them, but nobody knows quite where to put them! Some groups in arranging a service will 'get them out of the way' by having them right at the beginning of the service. Notices of the church's regular meetings are duplicated and handed out with the songbooks at the doors, but there are always one or two specials to be announced. One wants to let us know about a TEAR Fund prayer meeting, another is getting up a coach to go to a nearby town for the visit of a well-known speaker. After the notices there is a book spot given by one of our members who with a friend runs the Christian bookshop in town. From time to time she will recommend new publications or books suitable as background reading for the current series of 8 o'clock services.

After the book spot we focus our attention on the subject for the evening's teaching. A member of the group on duty reads an appropriate passage from the Bible and a short piece of drama is given to illustrate a point within the subject. Then comes a hymn during which the offering is taken and after that the address which is usually given by John Horner. This is normally twenty minutes of biblical exposition or some other Bible-based teaching.

This evening John has been asked for a laying on of hands. This will take place during the hymn after the address. The Spirit of God has been felt among us at this service, so an invitation is given to anyone who feels so led to join at the communion rail the person who has already asked for a ministry. Those who respond to this invitation may come for healing, for anointing for a particular task, for first-time commitment to Christ or rededication, for baptism in the Holy Spirit or for whatever the Spirit has prompted. About a dozen people respond to the invitation. Some mature Christians from the congregation come forward to assist in the ministry, and the music group leads the rest of the congregation in quiet praise and supplication. It is clear that God is dealing with his people in a variety of ways this evening. The ministry goes on for about half an hour. Each person receives counsel as well as the laying on of hands, and names are taken for the follow-up. There are some tears and much joy. In ones and twos people leave the communion rail and go through to the foyer where eventually almost the whole congregation assembles for fellowship and coffee. There is much excited sharing of what God is doing amongst us. As a conversation topic, the weather doesn't get a look in!

It is 10.40. Everyone except those responsible for locking up have gone home, and the foyer is stangely quiet. We gather up our books and coats and stand for a moment in the quiet dark of the chapel. A bastion of respectability? Perhaps not any more—but then, from the days of Simon Peter, Judas Iscariot and the publicans of Galilee, the disciples of Jesus were not noted for respectability. A bastion of tradition? Certainly—for tradition is a stream to follow not a pond to sit by. And the stream we follow is that living water which makes glad those who love the city of God.

Chapter 7

Poplars Christian Fellowship Worksop, Nottinghamshire

Peter Hardy

Poplars Christian Fellowship is set in the village of Carlton-in-Lindrick, just north of Worksop, and within commuting distance of the three urban centres of Doncaster, Sheffield and Rotherham. Since 1981 the congregation has tripled in size.

Poplars emphasises participation of all the believers in worship of God. It enjoys a varied expression of music and singing and, in fact, grew out of the ministry of a gospel singing group called Faith. Derek Wilkinson, the foundational pastor, and Norman Daniels make up the full-time leadership, ably supported by four elders, including Peter Hardy, author of this chapter.

Peter has served as elder since 1978. As head of careers and social education in the local comprehensive school, as a husband, and as a father of two young children, he is a busy man. He still finds occasional times, though, to enjoy climbing, walking, and reading history.

Over the years Jesus has laboured to instil into the fabric of this part of his body characteristics which have coloured every aspect of our lives and none more so than our worship. Today as we move deeper into the good things of God, sound relationships and obedience to the word of God challenge and stimulate fresh growth. So they did, too, when in the early seventies we were a handful of young believers barely filling the living room of Derek and Mo Wilkinson, where we shared God's Word and their time, coffee and home.

Our times of worship in those days would consist of gospel hymns—full of truth which even now many of us are just discovering truthfully—sharing of testimony and praying 'as the Spirit led'. As more and more of us came into the baptism of the Spirit, our meetings became in equal proportions longer and even more exciting. At that time more than a few of our young and eager fellowship could be cajoled into admitting that they had experimented with speaking in tongues. 'In the bath? Well I never!' 'Standing on your head? Not possible!' At the same time there emerged a vitality of spiritual life, a hunger for God's Word and a love for one another which can never be far from our Father's heart as he watches out jealously for his children and waits patiently for their heartfelt response to the love of his son Jesus.

Who Are We?

Poplars—a church of about 150—is based in a grouping of villages in the northernmost corner of Nottinghamshire. Most members of the church live in the villages of Carlton-in-Lindrick, Costhorpe, Langold and Oldcotes, whose overall population of 12,000 is made up of miners, farmers and a large number of families finding their employment in the neighbouring towns of Worksop, Mansfield, Retford, Chesterfield and the city of Sheffield. For some time the fellowship has used the local village hall in Carlton for congregational meetings. With a large open space and the flexibility of movable seating, we are able to have quite active times of worship—if necessary clearing all of the chairs to the sides of the hall for optimum use of space. Midweek meetings have been based on home groups in the past and undoubtedly will be again. In the meantime other groupings have come into existence to perform particular functions— praying for specific needs, spiritual warfare, preparing for evangelistic outreach, nurturing young converts and so on. In these situations worship, of course, plays an important part since each group is really the Church in microcosm.

Over the years many of those involved with Poplars have moved into the villages in order to be close to fellowship activity, but growth stimulated especially by the 1985 visit of Billy Graham to Sheffield has seen an influx of believers from Worksop and the Derbyshire mining villages of Creswell and Whitwell. With growth, change has of course been necessary, and we work on the precept Jesus taught that it doesn't pay to 'pour new wine into old wineskins' (Matt 9:17). Roy Turner, an elder in the church, has been used by the Lord on many occasions to set a challenge before us when, as change is required, this 'son of encouragement' has simply asked 'Whose church is this anyway?'

Under the care and direction of Derek and the eldership, every individual believer in the fellowship has been stimulated to answer this question for himself. It then becomes possible to consider for whom our worship is intended. If it is planned with only the people in mind, then we can organise and schedule it accordingly: Sunday meetings could be scored on a basis of how we did this morning, how we felt about the singing, whether we found it comfortable and acceptable or not. In I Chronicles 13 we find David reflecting in his actions, attitudes and failings which God has had to deal with in us in order to give us what we feel now is a healthier perspective on worship. It did seem right to the king and his people to bring the Ark of the Covenant—the symbol of the very presence and glory of God—into Jerusalem. Today we would all add our amens to this ideal as through our worship we too seek to bring in the presence and glory of God. But in his zeal David did the *right* thing *his* way. He set the Ark on an ox cart, and Uzzah's life was forfeit. It would be true to say that the Lord has had to show us His way—his glory doesn't belong on an ox cart, not even a charismatic one.

For years at Poplars, and still today, there has been a strong emphasis on the priesthood of all believers. In I Peter we are told clearly that we are a 'chosen people, a royal priesthood, a holy nation, a people belonging to God …' to 'declare the praises of him' (I Pet 2:9). Similarly we have been taught to 'eagerly desire spiritual gifts' (I Cor 14:1) and encouraged to offer our bodies 'as living sacrifices, holy and pleasing to God' (Rom 12:1). We are especially blessed to have responsive people who have a tremendous commitment to praise. But the Holy Spirit has had to mould us like clay to conform to the pattern God has in mind. The shape of worship now, it seems, needs to be organised and scheduled with *God* in mind—how did we do this morning in terms of how *he* felt about the singing and whether *he* found it comfortable or not. Commitment to this way of thinking has inevitably led to discomfort at times. Ultimately of course Satan objects! Teaching, love and determination to please God in fairly equal measures have served to keep many with us, but sadly—over the years—a few have left.

How Do We Worship?

Music and song have played an important part in the historical development of the fellowship. The small group of believers, meeting for simple prayer and Bible study, evolved from the ministry of a gospel singing group called 'Faith'. For 14 years, this group sang and played all over the country and also produced three albums. Initially, young people were drawn to spend time travelling with 'Faith' and to join in leisure pursuits together. Many of them committed their lives to Christ as a result of the group's ministry, and deep and lasting relationships were formed, many of which remain strong today. In the early days, the group travelled many miles for any opportunity to share the Gospel. Our driver, Ken Russon, once calculated that in one year we travelled 47,000 miles, which—even allowing for some exaggeration—meant that there was a lot of fairly close fellowship in those times. Gradually the group became more selective in taking on commitments. (There had been one occasion when we travelled 200 miles to sing two songs, and in a number of instances, we journeyed the 50 miles to Manchester for an evening session after work.)

As the years passed, we built relationships with several churches which continue to this day. We also developed musically and reached a stage where most of the material used was self-penned. Often, new songs would be written as a direct result of God's work in our lives. The fellowship grew to the point where Mo and Derek had to move house in order to contain the mid-week Bible study, and increasingly, numbers prohibited everyone travelling with Faith. The church was beginning to emerge and in May 1981, having heard the Lord clearly over a period of time, the ministry of Faith was laid down in order to give our efforts to the growing church in the community. Although much change was obviously required, many of the seeds sown in the early seventies were to germinate and develop later.

A consideration of a typical Sunday morning meeting might help to clarify the current situation and focus attention on how and why we arrived here as well as raising the issue of 'where do we go from here?' About an hour of a two-hour meeting is devoted specifically to blessing God. More and more we find the Holy Spirit leading us to concentrate on giving God glory, exalting him, praising him. Increasingly nowadays a worship indicator would point Godwards as we focus more on him and less on ourselves. The emphasis is moving away from the Body—the Bride being made ready—and towards the object of her love and concern: her eagerly awaited Bridegroom.

The importance of music and song in our worship has not diminished. During the first phase of the meeting, however, it is not unusual to find other forms of expression. Praying, shouting, clapping, waving, kneeling, mime, dance, drama, lying down, reading God's word, singing it, times of quiet (not many!) and allowing music to stir the people of God—*all* have their part to play. To this end, experimentation to some extent has been important—extravagance too. (Picture if you can the six elders singing and presenting a set dance—the Lord and they were blessed and most of the congregation fell about laughing! On another occasion, as a particular song was sung, a lady in the congregation simply poured out a bottle of expensive perfume. A large part of another meeting was devoted to the washing of the entire congregation's feet.)

The congregation is encouraged to participate fully, although the meeting nowadays is clearly seen to be led from the front. Over a period of time it emerged both from current demands and from careful study of Scripture that a 'charismatic knees up' was not quite what God had in mind for us. Scripture constantly serves to remind us that we are a prophetic people and as such need clear prophetic leadership under which we can blossom and flourish. It actually took some years for us to realise that although we are all called to be worshippers, some by their gift and example simply led the way forward in it. Their encouragement would often stimulate others to emulate them, even though for some of us there were moments of embarrassment as we became slowly used to unfamiliar expressions of worship. The Holy Spirit was leading us into greater intimacy with him! In these times of change, the leadership, too, has helped to maintain order and direction. In the early days with 12 in a meeting it was relatively simple to pull a meeting back on course. Now with 150 plus it is easier through good leadership to try to anticipate the pitfalls of digression rather than to go astray in the first place.

To bring order to the times of worship we needed to find clarity in the Word. If we as leaders could grasp the Holy Spirit's pattern, then God's order should follow, with its attendant security for the flock in our care. In our case I Chronicles 25 set out the scriptural order which we have sought to follow. Worship in the tabernacle was under the direction of the king and the commanders of the army, and at Poplars the worship is under the direct supervision of the eldership with one of the elders in oversight. We believe that in our corporate worship direction is important and, therefore, it has been a priority to maintain a prophetic edge at the leadership level.

A group meeting open to the whole church under the leadership of the recognised leader of worship takes place weekly to seek the Lord about the following Sunday's meeting. Often this is simply a time of worship in itself. What better way of preparing for worship than by worshipping? Within this group are a number of people who are recognised as progressing both in their personal spirituality and in their ability to take a public role as they grow in confidence and maturity. When Sunday comes, the leader of worship is prepared with a sense of where the Holy Spirit would like to take the people and is equipped with songs and Scriptures, visual aids, etc, to encourage the congregation to achieve the aims of the Spirit for the morning meeting. Preparation is important and encouraged—so the leader of worship may well be approached by members of the congregation during the week with suggestions of contributions. These vary: song, Scripture, drama, mime, a vision, a prophecy and so on. There is an argument that good preparation actually aids creative spontaneity, and this we want to encourage. Often the most beautiful times of worship leave us quite amazed at the freshness of the Holy Spirit—there is a zest amongst the people of God which like that of a freshly peeled lemon is distinctive, and impossible to imitate successfully or recapture. To encourage good order as these contributions are made in the meeting, we appoint an elder to sieve suggestions so that the actual leader of worship need not be distracted from the overall task of maintaining clarity and momentum. A degree of trust is obviously necessary, both in the giving and accepting of suggestions, and guidance as to what to do with them. In this way it is possible to bring in positive and 'spontaneous' contributions.

For instance, a prophecy may be brought to the meeting. The member of the congregation receiving the prophecy may at first be unsure and nervous of speaking a direct word. Checking it can help to verify the message or simply put it to rest before it can distract the meeting from the Holy Spirit's purpose. ('Thus says the Lord, "You brood of vipers!"' in the middle of the most beautiful singing in the Spirit may not be quite right!) If the speaker is asked to wait for the most opportune moment, that can also serve to bring out the best in the prophecy. A little more time brings greater clarity, a greater sense of readiness and receptivity on the part of the congregation to what God wants to say. Similarly we find that if it should be necessary to say 'no' to something, this is more easily done on a one-to-one basis rather than publicly. If on the other hand someone is encouraged but afraid to speak, he or she can be commended and, if necessary, given the support of caring leadership.

The New Testament abounds with instruction to the worshipper. For example, he should be first and foremost, as Paul exhorts him in Romans 'a living sacrifice' (Rom 12:1), worshipping to Jesus' own pattern 'in Spirit and in truth' (John 4:23). He should pray lifting up 'holy hands' (I Tim 2:8), and come to meetings eager to participate, bringing with him that special offering which is a gift of the Holy Spirit himself (I Cor 14:26). In this way he fulfils the instruction in Ephesians 5:19–20 to 'Speak to one another with psalms, hymns and spiritual songs. Sing and make music in your heart to the Lord, always giving thanks to God the Father for everything, in the name of our Lord Jesus Christ.' Though neither the Old nor the New Testament gives us strict patterns and models for worship, there were principles, and there was order. In the Old Testament the description of the order of David's Tabernacle illustrates family relationships at work and prophetic response to prophetic inspiration with men like Asaph, Heman and Jeduthun in charge, but accountable to the king himself. I Chronicles 25 finds these people on David's instructions

bringing their instrumental and vocal skills to maintain a
massive and continuous sacrifice of praise before the Lord.
In Hezekiah's day this order still prevailed, and skilled singers and musicians worked to provoke and encourage the
people. In II Chronicles 29:28 there is a glorious time in
which 'The whole assembly bowed in worship, while the
singers sang and the trumpeters played.' This continuous
worship is a foreshadowing of Revelation chapter 4, where
the living creatures before the throne day and night never
cease to say 'Holy, holy holy is the Lord God Almighty,
who was, and is, and is to come.' This moves the 24 elders to
fall down and worship (Rev 4:8–11).

Music in Worship

In 1984, continuing to find a way forward in worship, we
came to the conclusion that a firm foundation was required
if music and singing were to have the desired effect of stir-
ring the congregation. Over and over again in the Old Testament the musicians are found at the sharp end of Israel's
activity—often in battle. We saw the strategic nature of the
musician's role, and that without training and skill, little
headway could be made, though technical brilliance of
itself would not help win spiritual battles. Musicians in the
church were called together and a foundation of God's
Word laid for good musical practice. As a soldier does not
keep his rifle as a plaything, nor shoot for a hobby, so the
trumpeter and pianist, the guitarist and drummer involved
in worship need a clear calling if the music they produce is
to reach its full potential under the power of the Spirit to
help win spiritual battles, aid the pulling down of satanic
strongholds and release power among the people of God.

At this time it was pointed out that there have been many examples in secular battles when the musician has been out at the front. During World War I there were numerous occasions on which the first man 'over the top' was armed with bagpipes. This action—insane to the casual observer—brought men out armed with their weapons of destruction and spurred on to acts of great human courage by the sacrifice of the company musician. So, too, musicians can help to create a way forward for others to come, bearing spiritual weapons of prayer and intercession. We see this pattern clearly many times in the Old Testament. Joshua at Jericho (Josh 6), Gideon in his destruction of the Midianite army with just 300 men (Judg 7), and King Jehoshaphat in his defeat of the Moabites and Ammonites (II Chron 20) were all under direct instruction from the Lord to put musicians or singers to the front in battle. They were all winners!

A challenge had to be laid down. Are all who can play instruments fitted to play for worship? Is it better to work with a small number of people with their hearts in tune than with a whole orchestra of fine instrumentalists with hearts out of tune? When we gather together, are we seeking to create a work of art or a sacrifice of praise pleasing to God? From this point of challenge, we felt that progress could be made. If a person had counted the cost and come to a personal decision about his position in God's order of things then he could be relied upon to take his place within a group that would require—as in a military setting—discipline and commitment of a high order and a preparedness to sacrifice self, and if necessary professional musical pride, for the glory of God.

From the technical point of view, however, expertise was still required. Unless we were blessed with a leader in oversight who happened also to be a highly competent musician (which we were not!) then it was obvious that to stretch, encourage and train our musicians we would need the services of someone else who would also have the right heart for the job. Reports of situations in which the organist had successfully held up spiritual progress in worship for years by simply dictating to the leader, who was held over a barrel by the threat of resignation, made us concerned not to make a wrong choice! In the fellowship at Poplars we did indeed have a lady who had proved to be technically competent, able to lead and organise groups of singers and musicians and who at the same time displayed an anointing of the Spirit—rather than just a natural ability—in producing fine musical pieces, which had already enhanced the worship in the church.

Gina Gathercole was encouraged and publicly recognised as the instrument of the leadership in music to bring into being what could otherwise be only a very clever idea. Since that first meeting with musicians, progress has been made. Within a short time people in the church began to recognise a new dimension in the worship as the musicians gave a clearer lead. Regular practices were instituted, and the process of developing a group of skilled, sensitive and spiritually well tuned musicians continues. Although these sessions are essentially practical, teaching and encouragement to produce new music and songs also play their part.

Singing in Worship

Alongside the development of good musicianship we also had to consider a similar thrust with singers. Gina has done much work, and skilled singers have made a valuable contribution. In this department, Poplars is truly blessed in having a number of people who have proved their worth over many years. Mo Wilkinson, Pat Taylor and Rosie Evens in particular are competent and have had a great deal of experience in sharing the Gospel through song, as well as encouraging the Body of Christ and leading the worship by their fine example. Much effort is being given to training singers, encouraging skill and seeking opportunity for others who can also give a lead in the corporate worship of the church. Over a period of time, musicians and singers have been working together to produce anthems (set pieces which serve to stir the people), to help bring in new worship material by their firm lead and good example, and to minister to the body of Christ with songs which, in many instances, have been complemented by dance.

Worship and Discipline

Regularly on a Sunday now, the leader of worship is served by an appointed team of worshippers, musicians and singers working together to set a good example to the congregation. Discipline is an important part of this as the manner and appearance of the musicians sometimes communicates more than the music! The face and body often reflect the state of heart of the person concerned. It would seem only right that we should do as Jesus bids us in Matthew 5:16 and let our light shine before men that they might see our good deeds and praise our Father in heaven. Thus the musicians are expected to be punctual. The meeting begins at 10.30 a.m. and any musician not set up and ready to play by 10.20 a.m. at the latest must spend the morning in the congregation. If those who give a lead in worship are not on time, then it is difficult to expect the same of others. A good image is not seen as a religious façade but as a sound example.

When Samuel was sent out to anoint David king, he recognised the future leader, not only of the nation but of the worshipping priesthood, by his appearance. When the prophet saw the boy, he noticed that he was 'ruddy, with a fine appearance and handsome features' and immediately heard the Lord say 'Rise and anoint him; he is the one' (I Sam 16:12). Punctuality played its part too; one can only conjecture as to the course of history if the young lad keeping sheep had failed to come from the fields at his father's bidding.

To dwell on basic matters of discipline such as punctuality has proved to be very productive in the long term. We come back time and again to the importance of relationships with each other and the fact that, as a peculiar people, Christians need constantly to measure their conduct by the Word of God. In Nehemiah's day, the Davidic order was restored in Jerusalem at the dedication of the reconstructed walls. When the people gathered and worshipped 'by the book' the results were of greater consequence than anyone present could have imagined. Nehemiah 12:43 reports that 'The sound of rejoicing in Jerusalem could be heard far away.' True worship belongs only to the Lord (the man who reaches out to touch its glory for himself courts disaster) but its effects on the world are far reaching.

Where Do We Go from Here?

No glory belongs to Poplars, but it can be said truthfully that as we seek to move closer into the mind of God in worship, those as yet outside the Kingdom of God are affected. On a number of occasions visitors have come to salvation, not as a direct result of the Gospel being preached but as a result of being exposed to dynamic worship. We have been approached several times for help and guidance, and invitations have come in asking for a team to spend time teaching and leading worship in other fellowships. Religious platitudes and form without power do nothing for a hungry, empty world. Sadly the Church has often worn what Thom Gunn in his poem 'In Praise of Cities' called 'cosmetic light a fool could penetrate'. The genuinely worshipping church will have the young New Testament church's experience of daily having added to its numbers those who are being saved, and God can begin to enjoy the real fruit borne by his sacrificed son.

Looking to the future is certainly encouraging as ultimately we anticipate the Lord's return (with plenty to keep us busy until that should happen). Over the next few years we see a need to develop a strong, healthy church body in Carlton, worshipping in an even greater revelation of that which Jesus spoke of—Spirit and truth. To carry the work forward in Whitwell and amongst the group of people in Worksop who are currently worshipping with us, we need to develop and recognise new leadership. Since too there is a greater awareness that the fields are ripe for harvest, the church is reaching out to the world in evangelism more than ever before, with worship and creative expression in song, dance, drama playing a valuable role.

At least one dictionary defines that which is excellent as being 'of great value'. We believe that our worship is of great value to God, and the aim of our desire for greater excellence is to offer to him something which *he* will find to be truly acceptable. When we are 'out of sorts' with one another, it is difficult to experience the real heights as far as worship is concerned—it is in our unity that God commands the blessing. Worship is not for us; it is by us for him and must, like the Ark of the Covenant, be borne on the instruction of his Word. As in the past, the future—however exciting and fresh it may be—will, we suspect, be characterised by these two elements again and again. It would seem that, like the roots of poplar trees themselves, they go down deep and serve to bring up the sap of our spiritual well-being.

Chapter 8

St Mary's, Parish of Ballybeen Dundonald, Belfast

Norman Jardine

When Norman Jardine, minister of St. Mary's, came to the church in 1978, he found a community of believers some of whom had been influenced by the Renewal Mission of 1977, by visits from David Watson in the mid-seventies, and by the consequent springing up of numerous new Christian fellowships in the area. Members of the church worshipped in an atmosphere of 'freedom within a framework' and particularly enjoyed cross-fertilisation with the Dundonald Christian fellowship.

St Mary's strives to achieve worship that is liturgical yet living; God-directed, not man-centred; informal but not irreverent. In the strategic setting of a large Northern Ireland housing estate, it attracts many young people, some of whom have had little previous contact with a church.

Norman Jardine worked in both banking and textiles but subsequently left these careers to study first at Queen's University in Belfast, then at Trinity College, Bristol. He and and his wife Heather have three children; he enjoys walking, reading and all kinds of sports.

If you were to come along to St Mary's on a typical Sunday morning around 11.15 a.m., you would join a crowd of mainly local people also coming to worship. As you enter the church porch, you will be met at the door by a couple of people giving out worship books, and when you look at what you have received you will find there a copy of the Book of Common Prayer and the Church Hymnal (bound together), a Mission Praise book and a duplicated sheet containing a word of welcome, some details about 'forthcoming events' and the words for two or more songs. You may be aware that this large church porch was slightly over-full of groups of people chatting and laughing. When you enter the relatively new church building itself, you might become aware of a rather higher level of noise than you had expected. At the front of the church, on the building-wide chancel you will notice a collection of musical instruments and a group of people tuning up guitars or hunting out sheets of music from their folders.

By about 11.20 a.m. the musicians begin to settle down in their places. Between fifteen to twenty folks will then come up the church and occupy the choir seats; you will be aware that the choir has about twice the number of women than men and that about two thirds of the members are under 25 years of age. The choir are not robed, nor are they located somewhere separate from the congregation.

A few minutes before 11.30 a.m. the musicians will begin to play, but not perhaps the sort of church music you normally would hear before a service. Perhaps by now, however, you have become aware that, though there is a warm, friendly spirit about the place, these people are not merely here for social purposes. Like others who have visited us in the past, you too will sense from the 'atmosphere' and from the music that a great number of these people are genuinely here to worship God.

Around 11.30 a.m. those who are to lead the worship go to their prayer desks. By now the congregational chatter will have ended, and they are then invited to join in singing a chorus or a few verses of a hymn designed to help all there focus their thoughts and hearts on the God whom we have gathered to worship. This 'introit' is followed by a brief time of silence for people to pray, and then after a word of welcome the service will begin.

What you would then discover is that you are at a Church of Ireland worship service as you join in confession, prayers, responses, creed, etc. from the Book of Common Prayer. However, some things are different. The hymns are not all from the Church Hymnal, but you sing too from your Mission Praise book and perhaps also some of the hymns are on the duplicated notices sheet. There will be some of the hymns you have always known, some others which though obviously written many years ago you are not very familiar with and others that are very much new hymns. However you will be pleased to discover that people are actually singing, indeed some are apparently finding it an enjoyable experience. Some will have raised their hands in the air; perhaps others will be clapping as they sing.

As the worship progresses you will find that typically there will be the expected readings from both Old and New Testament and also several 'scriptural songs'—psalms or portions of psalms, canticles, etc. Most of the music, however, will be congregational rather than choral, song rather than chant. Sometimes the congregation may read the psalm together.

With a sermon of usually 25–30 minutes, the whole service will typically last about 1¼ hours. The congregation do not however all suddenly disappear to Sunday lunch, but rather groups will gather and chat. In this sense the worship ends as it began, with something of the horizontal dimension of worship expressed alongside the vertical.

So far I have sought to describe a typical Sunday morning in St Mary's Parish Church. If it leads you to ask the question—What is so different about that to have it included in this book?—my simple answer would be I do not know if it is so different. Rather we are an ordinary congregation of ordinary, mainly working-class people. The one thing I will say, however, is that many of us find that we meet with God as we worship. We find him there to uplift us and encourage us. Many of us find that worship is indeed something in which to participate fully and thus to enjoy.

How We Got to Where We Are

Let me explain a bit about the background of our parish and then set out some of the principles which lie behind the way we worship. Ballybeen estate, in which St Mary's is centrally located, is the second largest housing estate in Northern Ireland (pop. 10,000 approx.). The parish boundaries include about three-quarters of this estate, and also a few small private estates. The population is mainly Protestant and derived from re-development of East (mostly) and North Belfast, with also a significant number of families arriving in the early seventies as a result of the violence and intimidation in South and West Belfast. About a fifth of these families would claim allegiance to St Mary's as the local Church of Ireland.

St Mary's came into being in September 1965 as a daughter church of St Elizabeth's, Dundonald. The style of worship was always liturgical and prayer book but adapted to the fact that this was a new church of few members in a new area with no substantial churchgoing tradition. The worship life and organisations took place in a wooden dual-purpose hall. The congregation experienced steady if not spectacular growth, and by 1973 a large, purpose built dual-purpose hall had been opened.

Alongside these material developments things were also beginning to happen that would significantly affect the style of worship taking place. The 1970's were years which saw the Diocese of Down and Dromore, our diocese, engage in a 'Campaign of Renewal' led by Bishop George Quin. Involved in this were visits from church members of St Mary's and elsewhere, to churches in Coventry and then later to St Michael's, York (see chapter 10). Here many experienced a warmth, vitality and reality in worship which they wanted to see happen in their own congregations. The mid-70's saw some visits by David Watson and teams from St Michael's to our diocese, culminating in a 'Renewal Mission' in 1977. While many churches and clergy were unhappy with what they saw and heard, a significant number of people were deeply moved and challenged. St Mary's began to experience some of the effects of this in their worship, mainly through the use of what were then called 'renewal' songs.

What also began to happen, however, was the springing up of several 'fellowships' particularly in the North Down Area. Dundonald Fellowship, one such group, came into existence in the late 70's and drew together a large number of young Christians from different churches in the area to its worship gatherings and cell-groups. Here the young Christians discovered that worship of the Living God was as relevant today as it ever had been. Several of these young Christians were very gifted musically and began to employ their gifts in the worship.

When I arrived in the situation at the end of 1978, I found myself faced with the sort of 'problem' I was very glad to have. Around us were two groups of people: on the one hand this new church of St Mary's with quite a number of people open to change and ready to move on with the Lord, on the other hand this strong group of young Christians, many of whom were worshipping at St Mary's as well as in their fellowship, who had learnt a great deal about worship and the reality of an experience of God through worship.

My own spiritual background and experience had given me a vision for worship that could be described as a 'living liturgy' or as someone has described it 'freedom within a framework'. I was then, it seemed, in a situation that could enable something of that vision to be put into practice. As we began, slowly, to implement this, there were obviously some people who found it a painful process, but largely there was a spirit of co-operation and openness. Equally obviously there were some who were afraid about where all this would lead, while some of the young Christians were impatient at what they considered a much-too-slow process.

A minor crisis arose late in 1981 when our organist/choir-mistress had to resign because of ill health. Up to then she had been supportive towards, and co-operative with, what was happening, being in tune spiritually as well as musically. We were then faced with the question of what to do about a replacement organist. We had at this time several musicians in the congregation but no one who could take on the role of organist. Equally we were not at all happy with the idea of employing someone on a professional basis. We struggled on for a few months helped out by some good friends on Sundays, and putting the matter constantly before the Lord. His answer in that was to lead us to appoint a musical director, a former leader of Dundonald Fellowship, which by now had disbanded and encouraged its members to become active members of their local churches. A short time later the Lord brought to us a young lady music teacher, who wanted to use her music in worship. With these two now responsible for developing the music and the singing, we began to learn more new songs. This brought to a head some of the underlying tensions in the church over worship and led to several people no longer content to remain in the choir. Yet at the same time there was ongoing and increasing growth in the congregation.

Indeed this painful period had proved to be a major growth point in worship as we implemented more and more a style of worship that sought to be relevant to the people who were present in the congregation, yet which also retained the riches of Christian experience from past centuries. As others in the congregation caught the vision of living worship, so we found the Lord bringing to us individuals with music gifts to enable us to build a music/worship team. Within two years of our being in a position of having no pianist/organist we found we had four capable ones, plus several guitarists, a flautist, a drummer and one or two others who were learning brass instruments. The traffic, however, was not in one direction only because the end of 1984 saw our musical director move on to train for the ordained ministry and our organist go off to work with Scripture Union in the Irish Republic.

Where We Are Now

The Anglican concept of worship, according to Prefaces in the Book of Common Prayer and our new Alternative Prayer Book, is one of evolving patterns built on traditions reaching back through the centuries. We learn from this the fact that in worship we have never 'arrived', nor have we ever reached a position where we can say what we have is right for us now and will be always. The experience of our church, as of many others over the last couple of decades, has particularly been that of 'liturgical revision' and spiritual renewal leading to the emergence of multitudes (so it sometimes seems) of new songs of worship. Thus in describing where we in St Mary's are in our worship today I do no more than describe one stage in what will surely be a process of evolution.

Our pattern of worship services on an 'ordinary' Sunday would be a morning gathering of around 230–250 people. As stated earlier we retain the Book of Common Prayer in this worship service. Our evening service would average around 100 people, the average age being lower than for the morning. At this evening service we use the Alternative Prayer Book published in 1984. The emphasis of the two services would be slightly different—the morning being geared slightly more towards evangelism within the context of teaching; the evening being more directed towards deepening the spiritual life and experience of those who are committed.

Once a month we retain a 9.30 a.m. Communion service, straight Book of Common Prayer. Then later that morning our worship takes the form of a Family Service which draws in the biggest congregation of the month. In this we would aim to be more directly evangelistic and while we use visual aids, etc., to keep the children's attention, it is our purpose to speak clearly to the adults rather than simply having a 'Children's talk'.

On another Sunday we have a monthly evening Communion service using the new liturgy. This we find to be—for many of the congregation—the 'highlight' of the month's worship, yet to others it proves painful and sometimes disturbing. It is not the theological issues that cause the problems here but rather the differing attitudes where some see a Communion service as a celebration emphasising the corporate aspects of it, yet others see it as a meditation, thereby emphasising its individualistic aspects. As an Anglican I value both and seek to draw both together in the worship. In truth I find that here I come closest to experiencing my vision for worship that is living while liturgical, free yet built on a solid framework. Despite the problems I look forward each month to this evening Communion.

At all our worship services (except the once-a-month morning Communion) the worship is accompanied by a musical group. The group will vary from one week to another, but its core is now organ (electronic), piano, two or three guitars, drums. Other instruments we employ less regularly are synthesizer, flute, trumpet and horn. The group and choir are led by the pianist, again a music teacher who employs her gifts in also teaching others to play various instruments. The selection of hymn or songs is initially by the musical director, who submits the list to me, or to whoever may be leading the worship. The worship leader then changes or rearranges if need be, but time and again we discover how the Lord leads both in preparation; the hymns or songs fit the service theme so well.

The service will almost always be led by two people, by me as well as by one of our four lay readers. In addition to this, on occasions someone from the congregation will read the Scriptures or lead in prayer. During the evening Communion service we experimented for a while with congregational prayers, but the size and acoustics of the building worked against this. At present we appoint a few different members of the congregation to lead the prayers from the body of the church. We also leave room for members of the congregation to bring individuals in need before the Lord, both aloud and silently. Quite regularly we encourage people to speak during one of our services. This may be someone who had recently (though not too recently) come to faith in Jesus, or someone who has had a new experience of the Lord in their lives. Or perhaps some of our members who are serving the Lord elsewhere, or in training, speak of their experience when they come back to us for a break. Several times we have been able to welcome visitors from overseas and, if they are engaged in the Lord's work, hear and learn from them of the Lord at work abroad.

Some Principles Behind Our Worship

God Directed not Man-centred

This is surely first and foremost. When on occasions I have been asked to define worship the most I can say is that it is, for me, an expression of my love to God. For that reason I value—and we use—many new worship songs which are more obviously direct and simple expressions of love and adoration to God. Few of the songs we use or have used degenerate into sloppy or sentimental thoughts but so many, while simple, are sufficiently 'theological' to satisfy my head as well as my heart.

This desire to express our love for God in public worship has been, and remains, one of the prime motives for some of the changes in St Mary's. Sadly, too few of the older collections of hymns cater for this desire. Again, if we are to express our love for God as a congregation, we need to think deeply about the words we are using and also be warmed in our hearts as we sing. This then requires worship to be less rushed than is the case with a neat, slick, professional 'performance' of the liturgy. At times it also requires quiet, meditative music or singing, and silence.

In such worship, praise and thanksgiving should also be directed towards God. Here we find both old and new hymns give us words that express worship in respect to the great acts of God in salvation and in history, as well as for more personal reasons. Here the mood of joy and exuberance needs to be expressed, as was often the case in Old Testament worship (e.g. the opening words of Psalm 95:1–2 —the 'Venite', and many other references), and appears to be a feature of the worship of heaven (e.g. Rev 5:11–12a; 7:10). This leads us to conclude that singing is a vital part of worship and that we use our mouths to offer to God our 'sacrifice of praise' (Heb 13:15 cf. Ps 34:1; 63:5, etc.). For this mood we find the musical accompaniment very helpful in enabling us as a congregation to sing in a 'loud voice' unto the Lord, recognising that—as Dick Iverson says on one of his Bible Temple tapes—although 'the Lord is not deaf, neither is he nervous'.

These are two of the pressures for change that we have experienced over the past years in St Mary's. Significant numbers of people—both young and old, within the church and within Dundonald Fellowship—had been greatly touched by the Lord. As people were filled with a desire to express to God their love, praise, and thanksgiving, the pressure was on the wineskins of the liturgy either to adapt new contours or to burst open. To date, by God's grace, the wineskins themselves have been renewed rather than replaced and have taken such a shape as to contain the new wine. The benefit of this to the new wine is that while it remains in the wineskin it matures.

One reason I have taken so much time on this one principle is to counteract the impression that changing the wineskins (to keep to this metaphor) produces new wine. The idea is abroad that by changing liturgies or using new songs and musical accompaniment we can renew spiritual life and produce growth. Our experience has been that the relationship between change and growth is that growth produces change, rather than vice-versa. Although there is certainly growth in our church as a result of the new style of worship, the initial growth was Spirit-wrought and Spirit-given, and true growth must always be so.

One young man who recently gave his testimony at a guest service in the church said something that we as a church need constantly to keep in our minds—to warn us against thinking that by devising a more lively service we can attract people along to church. He had started coming regularly to St Mary's a few years ago, brought along by his girlfriend, who was a Christian. He enjoyed the worship and did not have to force himself to come. However, he was able to continue in that state of enjoying the worship and yet still being outside the Kingdom. The challenge to our worship is to keep it always God-directed and not man-centred, so as not to leave people comfortable with merely becoming churchgoers. By the grace of the Lord this particular young man was brought to a place of conviction of his need of Jesus and last summer entered the Kingdom.

Congregational Rather Than Choral

The Anglican concept of worship, with its use of prayer books, is designed to encourage a great deal of congregational participation. Unfortunately it is often the case that a large part of the congregation choose not to make use of this concept, while in other cases they may wish to participate but are prevented from doing so largely by music that requires quite a lot of expertise to sing. Behind some of the changes in the worship at St Mary's lies the need for the music and the liturgy to be such as to allow those who are wanting to worship and praise to join in with heart and mind.

In a new church like ours there were many who had little or no church-going experience. To expect such people to learn a style of music they encountered nowhere else in their life other than in church seemed to be a denial of the principle of worship in the language of the people and adapted to the culture of the people. We continue therefore to seek to have music and a worship style which give the opportunity for people to participate as fully as possible. It was this principle that lay behind our decision in 1981 to look to the Lord to raise up for us someone who had a musical gift to replace our organist. Our 'job specification' was for someone firstly in tune with the Lord, and secondly in tune with this principle of congregational music—obviously the quality of the music was important also. We believe the Lord has given us this. To my admittedly untutored ear, the music is technically of good quality but also simple enough and 'popular' enough to be of great use in helping the congregation to do more than 'make a joyful noise unto the Lord'. (Ps 66:1 AV)

Liturgical and Living

Arising out of the double fellowship situation I encountered at the beginning of my ministry, here was the problem of some members of the church who felt that the Prayer Book liturgy should be adhered to fully, whilst many of those who had recently either come to a living faith in Jesus or a renewal experience saw little or no value in liturgical forms. The way forward proved to be the developing of a worship style that used the liturgy as a framework to be built upon rather than as a cage to be trapped in. To the minds of some, the worship should serve the liturgy but in fact, to change the metaphor the liturgy should be the skeleton, the worship the flesh upon the bones. To quote from the Preface of the Alternative Prayer Book, 'This liturgy *becomes* worship when the people of God make the prayers their own prayers and turn in faith to God'.

As in any congregation there are still those who long for more freedom in worship and others who would like a return to the style of worship they knew in their younger days. Most of the congregation, however, seem to find freedom in worship and yet appreciate the way a liturgy—to quote the words of a gypsy evangelist to me some years ago —'lets you pack so much variety into one hour'. The congregation of St Mary's would quibble mainly with the 'one hour' bit!

Informal But Not Irreverent

St Mary's congregation began its life in a wooden, dual-purpose hall. The atmosphere was therefore always different from that of those congregations who meet in purpose-built structures. No one could be awed by a building in which, earlier in the week, he had played bowls or met with friends over a cup of tea. Only in 1984 did the congregation begin to meet for worship in a building set aside for worship alone. By this stage the congregation had adopted an informal approach to their gatherings and we survived the change-over.

This informality is not easy to define—it's easier 'felt than telt'—but it relaxes and opens us to expressing our emotions to God, as well as our thoughts. It seems to make worship in a church more a part of, rather than apart from, the rest of life. The dangers of over-informality are known, but in my assessment it does not lead automatically to irreverence. To some the general congregational chatter before a service is an irreverent distraction. However to identify reverence towards the Lord with silence or hushed voices, especially if that means that we do not greet the people with whom we are joining in worship, seems to be to read from tradition rather than scripture. In my ministry, the most silent of all the places I visit is the graveyard, the noisiest the maternity ward.

Informality does lead to irreverence when the chatter continues through the worship, the prayers, sermon etc. and to a large extent this happens less in St Mary's than in many other churches I know or visit. Also the worship in seeking to be God-directed does cause us to focus on the Majesty and Holiness of God as well as on his love and Fatherly goodness towards us.

This informality flows over into two areas that sometimes cause comment: the presence of children and the dress of the mainly young. Children (under 11) at a morning service probably number around 30–40. They are present with their families through the worship up to the sermon, when they go off for teaching specifically geared for them. Rarely do they cause any significant distraction. We also find that many of the teens and twenties come to church in casual dress, something unusual in Ulster church life. Some see this as a mark of irreverence and stress that they would not dress like that if they were going to meet with the Queen. But to so identify dress with reverence is again to read from tradition rather than Scripture and to forget that while in worship we are coming into the presence of the King of Kings, we are coming not as subjects but as sons and daughters of the one who is the King. And we are coming into the presence of the God who does not see as we see but who looks on the heart.

The Word and Worship

The attitude that views worship as the preliminaries to be quickly got through before we come to the Word is by no means uncommon in evangelical circles in Ulster. A W Tozer's remark that worship is the jewel missing in the evangelical church is sadly sometimes only too clearly demonstrated. On the other hand in many Church of Ireland churches the worship is so central and time so important that the Word must be limited to a 10–12 minute sermonette. We have sought to keep a balance between the worship and the Word, the result of which is simply that our services last longer.

A typical Sunday morning or evening diet of worship would include two Bible readings, several portions of sung Scripture, some songs of encouragement and exhortation addressed to one another about God (Eph 5:19; Col 3:16) and a sermon. As a preacher I find it so much easier to speak to a congregation who in their worship have sought already to meet with God and become open to God. Also by the time I have come to preach I have had my heart warmed by the presence of the Lord and am therefore so much the more ready to speak.

Worship should surely have a timeless quality about it, although this must never be abused by the worship leader's over-indulgence or the preacher being unnecessarily long-winded. We find morning worship normally lasting about 1¼ hours, evening services sometimes 1½ hours, and the evening Communion service sometimes closer to 2 hours. Rather than this having the effect of keeping people away we continue to experience steady growth at all services.

Weekday Worship

Worship, for both an individual and a congregation, should be a part of, rather than apart from, the rest of life. This, of course, must be worked out in many different ways. In respect of the more traditional definition of worship as praise, prayer and preaching, we find that our congregational worship continues in several ways throughout the week, especially in house groups and at our Saturday evening youth fellowship meeting. Also once a month we join with several other congregations in Dundonald for a 'praise service'. One helpful side effect of this co-operation is that members of the congregation can quickly learn new songs or new tunes to old songs. In addition, gifts of dance and drama were developed in such groups and later used in church services on special occasions. At present we find ourselves lacking leaders in these areas, but trust that we shall soon be able to develop and use them in the future.

The Heart of the Matter

As someone who has the privilege and joy of leading worship and preaching, I see a number of similarities in them. Both need careful preparation, not only of the material but also of the man. As an old preacher is reputed to have said regarding preparation for preaching: 'I read myself full, I think myself clear, I pray myself hot and I let myself go.' What applies there also applies to worship preparation— hence the need to have someone other than the preacher involved in leading worship.

However no matter how careful our preparation, come the moment before the worship begins, the best we have to offer God is a bundle of dry sticks. My prayer frequently at that time is 'Lord, set it all on fire to burn for you'. Living worship in the end is not simply a matter of mechanics or having all the right bits in the right places, but rather it must always be 'in Spirit and in truth'. Recognising that has been at the heart of our experience of renewal in worship in St Mary's.

To continue to believe it and act upon it will, we trust, lead us to experience constantly such living worship and to be led along the Lord's path for us in this primary purpose of congregational life.

Chapter 9

Clarendon Church
Brighton and Hove, Sussex

David Fellingham

Clarendon Church began in 1978 with fellowship meetings in a school gymnasium. As the fellowship grew to its present size of 800, leaders Terry Virgo, Henry Tyler and Dave Fellingham looked for another meeting place and found it in an old, run-down church building in Hove. The congregations now minister to the large urban centres of Brighton and Hove (300,000); to students at Brighton Polytechnic and Sussex University, and to many who come to the area either on holiday or for conferences.

Terry Virgo, well known as a speaker at and leader of the Downs Bible Week, was trained at the London Bible College and is the church's main leader along with Dave Fellingham. David's training in music at the University of Sussex makes him a well qualified director of music, and he works with Terry every year at the Downs Weeks in composing new songs for worship—all based on Scripture.

The training of these two men is reflected both in this chapter and in the worship of Clarendon Church. Terry, Dave and other members of the team work closely to ensure balance and freedom of expression. As a church, Clarendon bases its worship on New Covenant life (centred on the Spirit and the Word), which exceeds even the glories of David's tabernacle.

The towns of Brighton and Hove are situated on the Sussex coast just an hour by train from London. There is plenty to do—you can spend all your money in the wide selection of shops and department stores, take a trip along the sea front on Britain's oldest electric railway, look around the extraordinary Indo-Chinese Royal Pavilion, visit one of the town's many cinemas, restaurants, the Palace Pier or the Theatre Royal, or just while away the hours looking for a parking space! The population is a little less than 300,000, not including those studying at the University of Sussex and Brighton Polytechnic. Numbers are swelled seasonally by foreign language students, holiday makers and conference delegates.

Clarendon Church started as the Brighton and Hove Christian Fellowship in the autumn of 1978. By September 1979 the fellowship had outgrown the school gymnasium where it was meeting and moved into Clarendon Church in Hove. The building was erected in the 1860's, and during the latter part of the nineteenth century and into the first quarter of the twentieth century Clarendon was a flourishing evangelical mission. During the post-war years with the national decline in church attendances, the Clarendon congregation dwindled.

When the Brighton and Hove Christian Fellowship moved into this building, we found that it needed extensive renovation. Henry Tyler, one of the leaders, observed that the building spoke more of the reign of Queen Victoria than the reign of King Jesus. Over the years, extensive renovation and modernisation has taken place through the generous giving from the members on various gift days. In 1984 the work was completed. A dropped ceiling in the main hall, extensive redecoration, a house public address system, a built-in sound-mixing console, modern chairs instead of pews, have all helped to make the building not only look good but work well. Offices have been built in, side rooms and minor halls improved, a damp basement made workable for the young people and children. All this work reflects the lively Christian community which blends in with the building.

When we began to meet in the Clarendon building in 1979, the church had three full-time elders: Terry Virgo who was the leader, Henry Tyler, an experienced and much loved Bible teacher, and me. The congregation of over 100 seemed small in comparison with the size of our building. The church grew at a steady rate, and by the summer of 1984 the main hall was regularly filled with as many as 500 people. The leadership felt there was a need to plant another congregation, and in November 1984 the Brighton congregation began to meet separately from Clarendon. Some 120 people were planted out into a building that within two weeks became too small. In January 1985 a school hall was found for the Brighton congregation, and there are now approximately 400 people meeting there regularly on a Sunday. Recently we have brought both the congregations together on a Sunday morning in the famous Brighton Dome. It has been thrilling to use this historic venue for a significant gathering of the church. We have also occasionally used the modern Hove Town Hall for bringing the congregations together. With both the Clarendon building and the Brighton school hall full, the next phase was to divide again, and by September 1986 there were five congregations in Brighton and Hove, each with a full-time pastor and with the whole team under the leadership of Terry Virgo.

Over the last two years my role has been to establish the Brighton congregation and to keep a stability of ministry at home base while Terry and Henry have been travelling extensively. I will be moving between the five congregations, bringing encouragement and teaching and particularly developing praise and worship and the musical, creative side of church life.

At Clarendon it is our desire to see the Church of Jesus Christ restored and built according to the pattern of the New Testament. The church is geared to principles of restoration. Terry Virgo has written a book called *Restoration in the Church* (Kingsway: Eastbourne, 1985), which clearly outlines what he believes those principles to be. The main features of our church life are the emphasis on the Ephesians chapter 4 ministries (apostle, prophet, evangelist, pastor, teacher) and on plurality of eldership. There are currently eleven elders, seven of whom are full-time. To facilitate pastoral care, the church is broken down into smaller groups which we call house groups. The leader of each group is pastorally responsible for the people in his group and the house group leaders are overseen by the elders. Since we want to see all the manifestations of New Testament church life, evangelism, prayer, body ministry, the exercise of spiritual gifts and freedom in worship all play a significant part. It is in seeking to restore the church to the pattern of New Testament life and teaching that the church as a worshipping community is developing.

Worship and Scripture

The worship of God is a theme which runs through the whole of Scripture. The shorter Westminster Catechism states that the chief end of man is 'to worship God and enjoy him for ever'. If the concept of worship is so central to the Christian life, then we need to have understanding of what the Scriptures say on this subject. In the Old Testament the book of Psalms gives many insights into how we can worship God. In the New Testament Jesus speaks of the true worshippers as those who worship in Spirit and in truth. He said that the Father was seeking worshippers (John 4:23, 24).

In Philippians 3:3 Paul says that the true circumcised are those 'who worship by the Spirit of God, who glory in Christ Jesus, and who put no confidence in the flesh'. Paul also says that the natural outflow of the spirit-filled life is that we 'speak to one another with psalms, hymns and spiritual songs. Sing and make music in your heart to the Lord' (Eph 5:19). The same thought is repeated in Colossians 3:16: 'Let the word of Christ dwell in you richly as you teach and admonish one another with all wisdom, and as you sing psalms, hymns and spiritual songs with gratitude in your hearts to God'. The Word and the Spirit are essential ingredients of our worship. The preaching of the Word is an integral part of the worship. Biblical preaching draws us close to God, teaches us his ways, imparts faith for living and causes us to grow. It also enlarges our hearts for worship and often the preaching will lead into further times of worship.

In Romans 12:1 we are urged by the mercies of God to present our bodies a living and holy sacrifice acceptable to God, which is our spiritual service of worship. Paul shows us that worship is not just something we do on a Sunday but that our whole lives should be a fragrant aroma to the Lord as we serve him. Peter says in his first epistle that 'you are a chosen people, a royal priesthood, a holy nation, a people belonging to God, that you may declare the praises of him who called you out of darkness into his wonderful light'

(I Pet 2:9). We particularly do this as we worship. And the book of Revelation is full of worship to King Jesus with myriads bringing their songs of exaltation to the Lamb on the throne.

Since worship is such a central theme in biblical revelation, and since as our Father God longs for those who will worship him, and since worship is at the centre of New Testament church life—we believe at Clarendon that worship is a vital part of our life together. For us worship is not an optional extra but is an essential expression of our love and gratitude to God, both individually and corporately. God has not only commanded us to worship but also explains how we are to worship. It is for these reasons that we are seeking a Bible-based style of worship at Clarendon.

Worship at Clarendon

During the early years of the church our worship was recognisably charismatic with all its associated elements: raising of the hands, clapping, dancing, singing in the Spirit. Two significant influences on our worship were the Scripture songs of Dale and David Garrett and the musical *Come Together* by Jimmy and Carol Owens. Also in the late sixties and early seventies the *Capel Bible Week* then held at the Elim Bible College in Surrey was providing a large hearing for such new English worship songwriters as Graham Kendrick and Dave Bilborough. 'Jesus Stand Among Us' and 'Abba Father' were such songs from this era.

Worship at the Tabernacle of David

A significant development came in our worship when the songs that we were singing not only had praise and worship content but began to have a strong element of declaration. These songs were becoming a prophetic voice for what God was saying to his church. We began to learn about the restoration of David's tabernacle. In the Old Testament worship at the tabernacle of David was a significant time in Israel's spiritual history. It was a short period when there was worship and praise before the ark without the worshippers having to go through the ritual of blood sacrifices; in other words, it was an Old Testament glimpse of new covenant life. Many of the psalms were composed as expressions of worship at the tabernacle. Four thousand priests brought their worship offerings of praise day and night, and a hierarchy of musicians ministered under the direction of the chief musician. Some families were set apart for music making while others were trained in prophetic singing and with instruments. The atmosphere of the first few chapters of I Chronicles is alive with vitality and creativity as the people worshipped God before the ark, singing with musical accompaniment, clapping, shouting, dancing, kneeling, lying prostrate, singing prophetic songs, playing selahs (or instrumental breaks when people may meditate), songs for groups, songs sung antiphonally, songs of response from the congregation, instruments playing in the mood of the psalm, all joining together with a harmonious expression of praise. In the midst of it all God would manifest his presence.

Many years later, when the great days of David's tabernacle were long past and the nation was in spiritual decline, the prophet Amos prophesied that God would restore the

tabernacle of David (Amos 9:11). In Acts 16 we read how
the Council of Jerusalem met to discuss the legal question
of circumcision as it related to Christians. During the form-
ative years of the Early Church, there were those who tried
to insist on Old Testament laws and ritual, and circumcision
was a major issue. Thus in response to the debate the
Apostle James pointed out the reference in Amos to the restoration of the tabernacle and used this to show that the
time was now being fulfilled when men would live by grace
rather than law and ritual alone. David's tabernacle thus
prefigured the new age.

Imitating the Tabernacle Worship

We began to see the prophetic implication of these Scriptures for our worship and realised that there were levels of
creativity and expressions of worship which we had not yet
explored. We then began to use more musicians in our worship and began to develop a singing group to help give a
lead to the congregation. This opened up the way for exper-
imenting with ideas based on the music at the tabernacle of
David. In our musicians' rehearsals we tried to develop the
relationships between praise, declaration and worship. We
began to develop prophetic singing with songs of response
and to encourage the instrumentalists to work out selahs.
Sometimes we would take a psalm and try to set it in its original context. If the psalm exhorted us to clap our hands or
shout or kneel, then we would seek to do what the psalm
was directing. If there were repeated lines in the psalm we
would find a melodic hook which could be used as a response verse. This began to affect the way we worshipped
when the whole church was together. With more instru-

mentalists and singers to give a lead our congregational worship began to move away from singing one song after another. We began to recognise the importance of sensitivity to the Holy Spirit, and we began to place a much greater emphasis on the flow of the meeting. In our celebrations we now enjoy the freedom of worship in the way the Bible directs: corporate singing, raising of hands, clapping, dancing, shouting joyfully, kneeling, standing in silence and in awe are all ways in which we express worship to God. There are times of singing in the Spirit in which the whole congregation participates, times of prophetic singing by those who are able to minister in this gift, time for musicians to play creatively both in accompaniment and in selahs. There is opportunity for prophecy and the exercise of such spiritual gifts as the word of knowledge, exhortation, tongues and interpretation and healing, although in our celebrations, the size of the meeting makes it necessary for people to ask the leaders if they can participate. Within all this there is freedom for the Holy Spirit to do what he wants to do. Our basic structure is only a guideline—there is freedom for the delightful spontaneity of the Spirit, and each celebration is different.

In our celebrations we use an instrumental backing group of piano, synthesizer, bass, drums, rhythm and lead guitar with woodwind, brass and strings. The arrangements for the singers are carefully worked out, and although there is some improvisation, the parts are orchestrated. We have found that the more musicians being used the more essential it is to have written or worked out arrangements. Multiple improvisation only causes aural confusion. We also have a vocal lead of four to eight singers who sing parts which have been previously worked out.

Worship Leaders and Musicians

An important aspect of our life as a worshipping community is the training of worship leaders and musicians. Musical skill and character are the essential qualities for those who participate in the musical ministry at Clarendon. They must be prepared to practise on their instruments and be disciplined in the way they work. But at the same time we look for those who display a humble spirit, and we encourage them to develop their own relationship with God before they begin to contribute their music.

The role of worship leader is important because he must know when to encourage, when to exhort and also when to remain silent. The illustration I have used with our worship leaders to show them how far they should be involved in a meeting is to liken a worship meeting to a trip down river in a punt. Imagine the flow of the river and a punt full of people. The man with the pole will push the punt from its mooring, but it is the current of the river that gives the punt its momentum. If the river bends and the punt is driving towards the bank, the pole may be needed just to edge the punt back into the main stream. If there is an overhanging branch, he might warn his passengers to beware. The worship leader needs to be like this. He begins the meeting by focusing the people's attention on God, but once the meeting has begun, he is happy to allow the momentum of the Spirit to carry the meeting on. If something happens in the meeting that is outside the flow of the Spirit, then the leader should bring the meeting back on course.

The worship leader needs to know how much or how little to be involved. The key is for the leader to be relaxed, to be sensitive to the Spirit, to draw the people and not to drive them or falsely stir up emotion. Most of all he should be a worshipper himself. If the worship leader is preoccupied with God, the congregation will follow him. Those who lead in worship are not only those in leadership. If there is someone with a gift in this area, he will be encouraged to lead the worship, supervised by the elders. Sometimes the worship leaders and musicians will be drawn together for specific teaching.

Types of Worship

We are learning about the relationship between such different types of meeting as the celebration, the congregation and the cell, and we are seeking to develop a style of worship that is suitable for each meeting. We are trying not to over-emphasise technique because the essence of worship is that we give expression to our love for God. This is more a matter of the heart, not technique. However, there are certain principles that we teach our worship leaders to be aware of.

Celebrations In a large gathering where the emphasis is on celebration the musicians and singers give a prominent lead bringing in the principles we have learnt from studying the psalms and the account of the tabernacle of David. In this type of meeting the worship leader, in conjunction with the musicians, has the responsibility to keep the meeting moving. Thorough preparation is essential for leading a celebration. The worship leader is encouraged to prepare a list of songs which have a definite progression from one to the other. We find it helpful to begin with thanksgiving and praise, with songs that are focused towards God. From here the worship leader should have a sense of direction, and some sort of theme may emerge, such as the Kingship of

Christ, our redemption, spiritual warfare, or our fellowship one with another. There are many songs covering these themes, and the biggest danger is jumping from one to another without a sense of progression. In leading a celebration the worship leader is encouraged to have a sense of beginning, the middle and the end of worship, to have a sense where there is likely to be singing in the Spirit and to have scriptural comments which help the meeting to flow.

Certain practical problems need to be overcome with a large number of musicians taking part. The worship leader should communicate his expectations about the worship time to the musicians. They need to be aware of what songs are going to come next, and there should be discussion regarding key, tempo and the feel of the song. If the worship leader is an able musician he may be able to start songs in the right key but if not, the musicians take a more prominent lead. The role of the musicians is to accompany the singing, to provide a foundation sound for singing in the Spirit, to play sensitively behind any prophetic singing and occasionally to play on their own in the form of a selah. The singers are there to give a vocal lead to the congregation without dominating and also to be available to bring prophetic contributions in song.

Congregations When the church divided into two smaller congregations we expected that our worship would have a simpler approach, but the growth rate was so rapid that within a short time both congregations were operating in this celebratory style of worship. Now that we have broken down into five congregations, we are hoping the smaller meetings will allow us to simplify the musical accompaniment. In a congregational meeting there is much greater emphasis on each person being free to bring his or her contribution. It is in this setting that the musicians need to be sensitive to the 'each one hath a psalm, a hymn …' concept (I Cor 14:26 AV) and be prepared to follow what God is doing in the congregation, as well as giving the initiative in leading.

A congregational meeting requires a different type of leadership and a different approach from the musicians than does a celebration. The worship leader's role in the congregational meeting is to keep the meeting on course, still allowing for the people in the congregation to participate spontaneously in expressions of praise, spiritual gifts, prophetic songs and the starting up of songs. In a congregational meeting the musicians should see themselves as an integral part of the congregation, seeing their role as supportive rather than leading. Let us imagine that a song is started by a member of the congregation and it is in the wrong key. If there is a keyboard player or a guitarist who is capable of accompanying in this 'wrong' key, only that player plays for the first time through the song. At the end of the first time the key is changed to the right key, and all musicians join in. If the keyboard player or guitarist is unable to play in the key in which the song has spontaneously been started, it is better not to try but to wait until the song has been sung through once unaccompanied and then all come in on the right key. If the song has been pitched hopelesssly wrong we find it is better for the worship leader to stop proceedings and ask the musicians to give the right key. This can be done simply and effectively with minimal disruption to the flow of the meeting.

Cells In a house group meeting the worship is usually led by a guitarist and has a greater intimacy than that of a congregation or celebration. It can be a time for experimentation, and particularly for new songwriters to try out their material. We urge the leaders of worship in house groups to encourage as much participation as possible.

Special Worship Meetings Occasionally we have had special praise meetings which we have called warring praise. Psalm 149:6–8 says, 'May the praise of God be in their mouths and a double-edged sword in their hands, to inflict vengeance on the nations and punishment on the peoples, to bind their kings with fetters, their nobles with shackles of iron'. Praise is an important weapon in spiritual warfare.

In II Chronicles 20 there is a story of a great victory of Israel over their enemies. This must have been one of the strangest battles in history. Under the direction of the prophet Jahaziel, King Jehoshaphat gathered his army together and appointed the singers and musicians to lead the army out into battle. Then they began singing and praising the Lord, setting ambushes against the enemy. A great victory was won. After the battle the army returned to Jerusalem with great joy playing harps, lyres and trumpets.

When we worship we cast up a highway for God in the heavenly places (Psalm 68). At times we have gathered the whole church together and encouraged as many people as possible to bring their instruments. The purpose of the gathering has been to make a joyful noise to the Lord and to set up ambushes against the enemy. We have found that such times of praise have led us into specific intercession, particularly for national issues where injustice or evil are clearly apparent.

In our normal church prayer meeting worship plays a significant part before we come to intercession. The worship times in our prayer meeting are not led by any one person, and there is very little musical accompaniment. The simplicity and beauty of people's voices blending in harmony provide a good platform for intercession.

Worship also plays a significant part in our evangelistic

meetings. We have regular guest services where we preach the Gospel and pray to see people saved. These include times of worship, but we try to choose worship songs which have a Gospel content, and the worship leader gives simple explanations of the meanings of the songs. We often have musical and dramatic items which convey a simple message to the unbeliever.

Worship and Healing

During our times of praise and worship there have been many testimonies of God's healing power. Sometimes this has been through the exercise of the word of knowledge; a member of the congregation stands to describe a particular kind of illness, to which an individual responds and is then prayed for accordingly. At other times the presence of God has been so clearly felt that people have reached out to God, and without anyone praying specifically, God has healed them.

One particular example of this is the story of Dorothy, who had only a quarter of the sight in her left eye (at the top) a condition which she had endured for some years. She came to the guest service, focusing her mind on the Lord with no thought in her heart of healing. She had committed her condition to the Lord and left it there, but as she was standing worshipping it was as if all the lights came on; she felt sick and faint because of the brightness and suddenly became aware that she could see her husband standing to her left. After three months she had her sight checked, and the specialist found that she had perfect field of vision; she had been healed of the limitation, although she is still short-sighted. This is still the case some two years or more later.

There have been healings from eye and ear disorders, back problems, allergies and asthma. In April of 1986 Clarendon Church did a live worship album, and during the recording session, as we were worshipping, there were several healings.

Praise helps to strengthen faith, because when we praise we are focusing on God not on ourselves. One young lady had a mysterious illness which affected the strength in her legs. She had to walk on crutches, and the medical authorities were mystified. In the context of pastoral care from her house group leader she was encouraged, like Sarah the wife of Abraham, to grow strong in faith by considering the faithfulness of God. Faith grew in her heart, and she was able to throw the crutches away. Although this did not happen in a worship meeting, this is a good example of growing strong in faith through praising the Lord.

Worship and New Songs

A significant feature of what God is doing today in the Church is the number of new songs there are to sing. Keeping abreast of most recent worship songs can be difficult. Our purpose in trying to learn new songs is not for the sake of learning something new, but when people are corporately expressing a truth that God is speaking to his church, faith can be built into their hearts, especially when they are singing words of Scripture. Many of the new songs give a prophetic insight that highlights neglected truths of what God is saying to today's church. We have found that at particular times international songwriters have been independently writing songs on similar themes.

On many occasions a spirit of revelation has come upon

the congregation as they have sung the truth. There was one memorable time when we were singing the song from Ephesians 1:3–5: 'Blessed be the God and Father of our Lord Jesus Christ' (NASB) when such a spirit of revelation came upon us that we were singing this one verse of Scripture for some 20 minutes. The sense of God's presence with us meant that revelation dawned upon many about their position in Christ. That night many pastoral problems were resolved by God as people gained knowledge of their sonship and security in Christ.

To keep up with the new songs, we find it more effective to use an overhead projector than songbooks which rapidly become outdated. (We do of course gain the necessary copyright permission for use of songs.) Those who work the overhead projector have an important role in the worship. They need to find a song quickly, to place it on the screen so that all can participate, and visitors and strangers to our style of worship do not feel excluded.

We have also given a new lease of life to many of the great hymns of the past. Such hymns as 'The God of Abraham Praise' and 'Join all the Glorious Names' are packed full of truth. Without in any way detracting from the content of these hymns we have sought to give a more contemporary flavour to such majestic tunes.

At Clarendon we see worship as an integral part of church life. It is our aim for all members to present themselves to God as living sacrifices by their spiritual service of worship (Rom 12:1). Thus worship is a lifestyle in which we grow to maturity. It is our aim for all members to participate in the worshipping community by expressing their love and devotion to God and their fellowship one with another. We are seeking to develop creativity and encourage others to exercise their gifts in order that we might find a whole variety of ways of expressing our worship. We are seeking to be open to the Holy Spirit to teach us and to prevent us from creating our own new and inflexible structure. We want constantly to be open to the Holy Spirit in keeping a freshness in the way we worship. Our aim is to be a community who worship in Spirit and in truth.

Chapter 10

St Michael-le-Belfrey York

Andrew Maries

St Michael-le-Belfrey is situated in the centre of the historic city of York in a largely commercial area. Members of the congregation come from all over the city to fill a church that was once described as redundant but which now rings with enthusiastic worship.

Incorporated in the St Michael's worship is a unique mix of form and freedom, structure and spontaneity. Participation of all members, including children, especially in drama, music, and dance, is essential to the church's approach to God. Under the vicar, Graham Cray, a corporate leadership of 17 elders serves the congregation. Among these is Andrew Maries, author of this chapter, who is full-time music director.

Andrew has written elsewhere about worship—in One Heart, One Voice, *published by Hodder and Stoughton in 1986. He and his wife Alicia have three children. Although he plays the organ, he is mainly known as an oboist. His love of music and his desire to worship God through music shine clearly from this chapter.*

At the heart of the historic city of York stands a rather squat, gloomy building just across the road from the cathedral. St Michael-le-Belfrey gets its strange name from its proximity to the Minster bell tower. Its own bell hangs in a little turret above the door—the bell swinging one way and the clapper the other! St Michael's claim to fame used to be that Guy Fawkes, perpetrator of the Gunpowder Plot, was baptised in the church in 1570. These days, St Michael's is known for a different kind of explosive—the 'dynamis' or renewing power of the Holy Spirit.

Morning Family Service

Of the thousands of visitors who converge on this beautiful city every year the majority have their eye on the glories of the Minster. Not surprisingly most people overlook the uninteresting building next door. But on this particular Sunday morning in June a most unusual sight is happening on its forecourt. A large circle of adults and children is singing and dancing, accompanied by a couple of guitars, a double bass and a wheezy accordion. The lively music and the joy on the faces of the participants encourage some of the visitors to come in closer. When the music stops, some are drawn inside with the large chattering crowd.

Once inside, they are surprised by a number of things. For one thing, the interior of the church isn't gloomy; it's light and spacious. Fine medieval architecture and stained glass abound, while colourful banners hang from the pillars. All sorts of people, young and old, are leaning over the pews greeting one another, exchanging news. There must be six or seven hundred there. At the front, others are making final preparations: the musicians are tuning, the organ begins to play softly, and one of the leaders comes forward and encourages people to find their seats and begin to prepare themselves for worship, as the service is just about to start. Five minutes later the congregation stands, the clergy enter, and the service officially begins.

The first item is the familiar hymn 'Praise my soul the King of heaven'. The visitors begin to feel a little more at home. Although the organ is playing, they can hear some other instruments too. With a craning of necks, they can just see a small band of children playing violins, recorders, clarinets and a guitar. There's a conductor, and over the other side, across what looks like a stage, a small group of singers stands behind microphones.

After a simple prayer of confession, the service leader encourages everyone to turn round and greet one another. A great hub-bub breaks out and the visitors, rather taken aback, are welcomed and introduced to those all round them. Meanwhile, the singers have mounted the stage, and people are being asked to sit down. It's time to hand out the birthday cards. Three or four children have chosen songs and stay on the stage with other small volunteers who are invited up to join the singing. Several choruses have energetic actions, and in 'The Butterfly Song', everyone has a go at being butterflies, kangaroos and elephants! Young and old join enthusiastically in the singing which becomes quieter and more reflective towards the end of the time. The visitors sense a reality and intimacy in this new style of worship. It feels rather strange and a little threatening, and yet there are warmth and relaxation too. It's also been fun, something they hadn't associated with church.

A simple question-and-answer creed follows, then another song. This has guitar and piano accompaniment, and the orchestra again plays along. However, another unusual thing is happening. Two or three adults and about fifteen boys and girls gather on the stage and perform a dance. The song called 'God is Our Father' has everyone on the stage waving imaginary tambourines, clapping hands and dancing round in a circle.

Next come some prayers led by a young family. Father introduces and each of the three children reads a little prayer which they have obviously composed themselves. The smallest gets a bit stuck and has to be helped out by Mum, who then sums things up.

Back to familiar territory with the offertory hymn, but whatever is happening now? The most enormous white screen is being manœuvred round a pillar and onto the stage! Surely they're not going to have a film in the middle of the service? A teenager comes to the microphone and reads a passage from the Bible. One of the ministers moves to the pulpit.

It turns out that the screen is for illustrating the talk with colourful and humourous transparencies. The title is 'Our Father in Heaven' and the visitors find much which relates to them as adults but which also engages the children. The preacher asks many questions as he goes along and has a good rapport with his audience.

In ten to fifteen minutes the talk concludes with prayer, and the service ends with another song called 'Sing to our Father'. After the blessing the congregation is dismissed, and the friendly hub-bub resumes. The whole thing has lasted just over an hour.

Evening Service

At this point we'll leave our imaginary visitors chatting to their neighbours. One real visitor who came recently was our archdeacon. He visited the evening service. Afterwards he asked the curate if it was like this all the time? 'No', said the curate, 'Only once a week on a Sunday!'

Like the family service, the evening service shares many of

the same ingredients as the morning but set in an adult context. For example, dance is often used outside before services in the summer months. Men and women are involved together in this excellent way of bringing the life we share as a church out into the city. Israeli dances are particularly useful, providing corporate activity and great fun.

Inside, the same warmth and sense of family pervades but with many teenagers in evidence rather than small children. Instead of the singing group, a larger choir now takes over the musical lead. New banners are put up to match the theme of the service, and drama is used occasionally to illustrate the sermon. Dance reappears frequently accompanying some of the more modern songs. Both sexes again take part with people drawn from the regular dance group. The movement combines grace with naturalness. Dance, like a descant in movement, will often heighten and personalise the worship, drawing the congregation into a deeper awareness of God in their midst. Its visual impact in an otherwise static service is refreshing and uplifting.

Whereas the family service is based on a form provided by one of the Anglican church societies, the evening service follows the new form of evening prayer. It has a definite structure with set responses and a rhythm of readings and music. Traditional hymns and the occasional anthem are balanced with more contemporary styles of music. The sermon is the main focus of the teaching. We try to balance structure with spontaneity and usually include an informal time of praise. This may come at various points in the service, depending on what seems appropriate. It could come after the liturgical response 'and our mouth shall proclaim your praise' at the beginning, before the prayers or later on before the sermon. It could provide a time of response in worship after the sermon as a conclusion to the service.

This time is usually led by two members of the choir in conjunction with the service leader. They have equal responsibility in leading the worship with him. Beginning with two or three lively, positive songs, an atmosphere of faith and expectancy is consciously built by the worship leaders as one song flows from another. Through this means an openness and receptivity in worship are established, attitudes often lacking in the stop/start features of many services. Leading informal worship is a skilled task, and those involved must constantly be aware of the power music has to manipulate people emotionally: we may seek to encourage people to open up to God in worship, but we cannot engineer the Holy Spirit.

This awareness of natural and spiritual planes is especially important when evaluating particular spiritual gifts which may well be offered in such a time. Often someone may come forward with a word that they believe God wants to say to the congregation. In such a large setting it's important that one of the worship leaders, probably the service leader, has the opportunity to assess this before it is presented to the congregation. This applies to other gifts such as mental pictures, words of knowledge (perhaps that God desires to heal a hidden need), and testimony. Sometimes a prophecy may be given in improvised song, other times the beautiful phenomenon of singing in the Spirit, where the whole congregation improvise their own melodies in tongues, may take place. Silence is an important ingredient, too. If worship is to be a dialogue with God, we must also take time to listen. The temptation is always to fill in uncomfortable gaps and push on to the next activity. How much we still have to learn in this area. Services usually last about one and three quarter hours in the evening unless we have a full Communion service which may be two hours, sometimes more.

Establishing Worship Patterns

While many visitors might find our worship very new and strange, it has been our norm for many years now. Gradually, we have tried to acquire the skill for walking that difficult tightrope between the liturgical requirements of an historic denomination and the freedom and spontaneity characteristic of renewal. This has been a creative tension, and finding new ways to maintain the freshness of routine Sunday worship has been an unending and inexhaustible task.

However, the excitement of the new has to be given over to a deepening of spiritual life in the everyday scene. Flitting from one new thing to the next does not produce growth and maturity. The first flush of enthusiasm eventually dissipates in the pain of growing together in love. We have tried to bring these darker experiences into worship too. Life is not constant joy and light, and we would be less than honest if we could not express weakness and failure when we gather together in worship. The painful, difficult times have in fact been the times of strongest growth. God has used them to challenge us and bring us back to renewal—a constant process of repentance, change and obedience.

The Watsons' Ministry

This history began for us in 1965 when David and Anne Watson moved to York to take over the nearly redundant church of St Cuthbert's for a trial period of one year. David confidently asserted to the authorities that if anyone preached a clear and faithful Gospel the church would soon be full.

It was no easy task—there was a handful of people at each service and both he and Anne needed much faith to see their vision as more than an idle boast. They began by setting aside one day a week to fast and pray. Next came a mid-week fellowship for prayer and Bible study in their house, at first attended by two old ladies and a dog! A weekly family service followed, planned with the intention of reaching young families.

Soon the congregation began to grow attracting people from all over the city and surrounding area. The focus of spiritual life centred on the fellowship meetings. Here David laid a strong foundation for spiritual growth through his excellent, systematic exposition of the Bible. Many people came to personal faith through his teaching. Furthermore, people were encouraged to learn more of the renewing work of the Holy Spirit, and many experienced the touch of God's power in their lives, confirming and authenticating their faith.

These were exciting days. Within a few years the fellowship, which had originally occupied one room in the rectory, had spread via relays to nearly every room in the house. Sunday services were equally alive with the hum and expectancy of the small crowded church. In the family service, the highlight became the talk which David illustrated with ingenious visual aids each week. Similarly, his masterful exposition of the Scriptures in the evening service was eagerly anticipated.

In 1969 the midweek fellowship gratefully moved into a rented hall near the church. It was now possible for the committed membership to meet all together in one place and begin to identify itself as the Body of Christ gathered for praise, prayer and the study of God's Word. To this date the concept of the church as the Body of Christ had had little significance with only 'churchy' connotations. Now, many aspects of this corporate life could be nurtured, and all the spiritual gifts could be weighed and corrected in the presence of the whole. Praise could be more focused in the gathering of all in worship of God and the musicians motivated to see this as a real ministry and service to the Body.

When new songs began to be introduced from similar renewal movements all over the world, it soon became apparent that a small group of musicians was needed to help lead this music on a regular basis. This was especially true when these songs were included in Sunday services, and the organ was found not to be the ideal accompaniment.

But by 1973 the congregation had moved to the larger church of St Michael-le-Belfrey (also threatened with redundancy); the organist had resigned and I had begun to take over as music director. In that summer we called together all those who had an interest in the music and worship and spent a day at a local conference centre. David gave some teaching on the principles of praise, looking at its significance in the Bible, and time was spent in prayer and discussion over what we felt God wanted for our church. A calling and commitment to lead worship were emphasised over and above musical expertise, and a group of some 15 people were drawn together in the following months.

Anne Watson's presence in the group stimulated and guided this vision initially until the time came when she felt she could leave it safely in our hands. Soon the group was operating at the fellowship and at both Sunday services each week. There was no other musical lead, and a high level of commitment was required. Worship, prayer and the sharing of personal needs and encouragements were made central features of our weekly meetings. Through this our ministry developed an integrity and reality which in turn encouraged the whole Body to join with us in entering God's presence in worship.

As soon as Anne left the singing group, she went off to undergird the development of dance. A visit from a Canadian group called 'Shekinah' in 1974 gave great vision and impetus for the use of dance in worship. Soon dance became a regular feature in the services, and the dance group, like the singing group, formed a strong commitment to their ministry and to one another.

When the Holy Spirit is active in a fellowship many gifts will be released, not least in the creative arts. The singing and dance groups were expressions of this renewal. Not surprisingly, a banner group soon came into existence. One girl began to use her artistic gifts to make prophetic banners which would help interpret the themes of seasons and services; she drew others round her in the process. We also began to use drama as a powerful means of communication both at home and in the many missions which David Watson led all over the country. This ultimately led to the formation of Riding Lights, a professional Christian theatre company using St Michael's as its base.

Unity and Variety

The richness and variety of our worship life were made possible by the fact that many of those who led or took part in these groups lived in households or communities within the church. This ethos of 'community' continues to influence fundamentally the life and ministry of our worship groups to this day, even though most of the households have long since disbanded. At its heart is the belief that, if we are to express the life of God in worship (as well as in every aspect of church life), then love and unity must be at the centre of all that we do. Living together in openness and trust helped many of us to deepen our personal faith and to begin to know ourselves through the joys and pains involved at a level few of us would have experienced in any other way. It also released many like myself to take on leadership of various aspects of our life which would otherwise have been prohibitive in time or cost. The deepening of relationships among a smaller core acted as a catalyst for the whole church, and that basic understanding of the importance of our relationships has not vanished as we have moved from living under the same roof to a broader and more inclusive view of 'community'.

Another aspect of our worship life has been our children's ministry. There is a strong belief that children should participate with us in worship, not as inferior, second-class people, but as children of God in their own right. They are our brothers and sisters and should be treated as such. God is able to touch and move in their lives just as he is in ours.

Consequently children have always had an integral part in the worship of our family service. They are not hived off for our convenience while we get on with the serious stuff! Instead, they participate fully doing readings, prayers, singing and playing, performing drama and taking the collection. We do not have a Sunday School but instead have a meeting early on a Friday evening called the 'children's workshop'. It aims to encourage our children to discover each other as brothers and sisters in Christ, to learn to love and trust each other and to expect God to speak to and act through them in their daily lives. Older children then move onto Pathfinders and an older group called 'Eureka'.

The discovery that we are all *equally* members of the Body of Christ has been very important in our development. In the early days of St Cuthbert's, David Watson provided in his ministry and personality a focus for the whole life of the church. He was certainly aware of the potential dangers of this, and critics were not slow to point them out at the time. However, we gradually discovered that each one of us had a part to play in this body and began to take on more responsibility for its different functions. Those of us who lived with

David found that he too had weaknesses. The mouth was no more special than the hand or the foot—just different. If some of us took responsibility lightly and were only half committed, then the whole body suffered. It mattered if you missed a singing group practice or didn't bother to turn up on a Sunday. If the preacher had to be there, so had the worship leaders! David's willingness to make himself vulnerable by sharing his ministry and leadership with others encouraged this sense of equal responsibility enormously. Many of us came into spiritual maturity and discovered our leadership potential as a result: something which would have been denied us had he held on tightly to the reins. Surely there is a very important lesson here for many of our church leaders.

Reconciliation

God has also taught us about *reconciliation*. We have been reconciled to God through the death of Jesus on the cross, but also reconciled to one another. This horizontal aspect is as important as the vertical and in fact validates our love for God (I John 4:20). We share the same Spirit and are part of the same Body. Much of the ministry of St Michael's has been involved in reconciliation. David Watson's particular genius was his ability to relate to people of many different denominations and backgrounds and to bring them together in their common desire for renewal. Our learning to accept one another and work out our differences taught us much about accepting others from outside our fellowship. In St Cuthbert's days we were called the 'Cave of Adullam' by the Archbishop of York, a reference to the place where all King David's malcontents hung out. Our move into the more public and more gracious setting of St Michael's right in the heart of the city taught us to assume greater responsibility and maturity in our relationships with other churches. An increasing number of visitors for renewal weeks broadened our horizons and we learnt much from the different perspectives they brought to us.

Our worship grew with us, broadening and combining many different elements. It is still strongly participatory and personal, which stems from our evangelical tradition. At the same time the eucharist has had increasing significance for us as we have discovered ourselves as the Body of Christ. Our worship is also innovative. We experiment constantly with new styles and patterns of worship, changing the order and ingredients in a service to fit in with what we feel the Holy Spirit wishes to do at a particular time. Services are planned by a small 'worship committee' which meets every week and has representatives from the different aspects of our worship life. Together we choose hymns and songs, dances and banners and talk through issues which affect our worship week by week. This corporate sharing of responsibility keeps us in touch with the heartbeat of the fellowship and ensures that our form of worship always serves the body rather than individual taste or preference.

The reconciliation we find as young and old, businessman and unemployed, labourer and university graduate is reflected in our worship. Contemporary songs rub shoulders with traditional hymns and anthems. Exuberant praise, even humour and applause, blend with silence and contemplation. All make a rich and varied crown of worship to glorify our God.

Choir and Congregation

One interesting illustration of this has been the development of a choir. The singing group operated successfully from 1973 to 1979 but latterly began to lose the edge of its ministry. With the advent of dance it lost intimate contact with the congregation, and its small membership became increasingly burdened with the commitment. Our repertoire of unison guitar songs had also become limiting, and there was a desire to explore and expand our musical horizons into choral and traditional fields. We were also meeting many people from other churches who, while possessing choirs, had little or no vision for their use. My own contacts with Betty Pulkingham and the Church of the Redeemer in Houston had encouraged me to believe that it was possible to see a renewal of worship using every style of music with one all-purpose music group. 'Choir' was the obvious name for it, and after prayer and discussion we bravely changed horses at the end of 1979.

The choir exists to serve the evening service, but volunteers join with others from the congregation to form the smaller singing group which I described in the family service. Despite many initial problems, the choir has proved itself to be a wonderfully fruitful place for growth and development. Now numbering almost forty, the group maintains the fundamental vision of its predecessor while involving many more in leadership.

The building bricks of the choir are its small cell groups in which members gather for prayer and fellowship within the choir practice every other week. The leaders of these groups make up a pastoral committee which meets to share and discuss the leadership with me as musical director. Alternate weeks begin with a general time of praise and worship often including some teaching and personal ministry where we may gather round an individual to pray and lay hands on him. There is no point in the pursuit of musical excellence in a worship group if individual members are left hurting and uncared for. Usually these activities occupy about half of our two-and-a-half-hour practice time. but occasionally it may be important to spend longer building the life of the group. This, after all, is where the integrity of our leadership of worship stems. Not every church has the resources to do what we have done. However, we too started small, and it is the *principles* of worship and sharing which are the most important; these can be translated into groups and churches of any size.

The varied nature of the congregation is, of course, reflected in the make-up of the choir. Classical musicians fraternize with pop lovers. Some read music, others do not. Vocal ability is also varied. It all provides a great educational experience as we learn to blend our different gifts and personalities as one. The strong must learn to support the weak. Gifts must be used to serve and build up the Body, not promote personal ends.

In this accepting environment new gifts begin to emerge. Many surprises are in store when people who felt they had nothing to offer gradually find that they have a gift for song writing or guitar playing, introducing songs or praying with people. It has been so thrilling to see our own experience in worship expressed in original music created by our own people. It may not be the most polished or expert available, but it is part of us.

The seeds of God's Kingdom may seem very small and insignificant at first, but they grow in amazing ways. They need nurturing in the fertile soils of prayer, Bible study, the power of the Spirit, and the building of ordinary lives into a living organism. Particularly important in enabling this growth are the quality and flexibility of leadership and the availability and commitment of the members. Any spiritual growth demands a cost, particularly if the church is pioneering new fields. For us, the old dictum 'joy and pain are woven fine' has been true. Hebrews 13:15 encourages us to offer to the Lord a sacrifice of praise. Being involved in the ministry of worship has involved costly sacrifice, often for just a few. My own ministry in music would not have developed had the Watsons not had a vision for the priority of worship. They shared their lives and their resources with me in our household to make it possible.

There have been many battles too. The beginning of the music group aroused much criticism from some who saw us as exalting ourselves. Later, the idea of a choir was anathema for others who considered it a tool of the devil! Dance similarly brought problems of acceptance for those who found it immensely threatening and difficult to cope with. But this is to be expected. Leading worship is a vulnerable activity. Worship leaders are the standard bearers going out before the army and raising the banner of the Lord in the face of the enemy. They should expect spiritual attack in many forms.

But despite the battles, it has been such a privilege to enjoy the presence of God together in our worship, and to see him constantly moving us forward into new vistas, new challenges. As to the future, we believe God is turning us outwards to share the life he has given us more widely. We pray that the seeds of renewal, which have borne so much fruit in our own lives, may increasingly stimulate the life of the wider church and also the secular life of our city. We see little clouds on the horizon but as yet await the rain.

What Is World Vision?

World Vision is a major Christian relief and development agency, founded over 35 years ago. World Vision now helps the hungry, the homeless, the sick and the poor in over 80 countries worldwide.

World Vision is international, interdenominational and has no political affiliation, working wherever possible through local churches and community leaders in close co-operation with the United Nations and other international relief agencies.

Childcare sponsorship is an important part of World Vision's Christian work. Over 400,000 children are currently being cared for in over 3,500 projects.

Sponsors in Europe and around the world are helping thousands of needy children by supplying food, clothing, medical care and schooling. These children usually live with their families although some are in schools or homes. Development and training are usually offered to the communities where the sponsored children live so that whole families can become self-reliant.

World Vision is able to respond with immediate and appropriate relief in crisis situations such as famines, floods, earthquakes and wars. Hundreds of thousands have been saved in Africa through feeding and medical centres. Other projects include cyclone relief for Bangladesh, relief work in Lebanon and medical assistance for Kampuchea.

Over 500 community development projects in 50 countries are helping people to help themselves towards a healthier and more stable future. These projects include agricultural and vocational training, improvements in health care and nutrition (especially for mothers and babies), instruction in hygiene, literacy classes for children and adults, development of clean water supplies and village leadership training.

World Vision's approach to aid is integrated in the sense

that we believe in helping every aspect of a person's life and needs. We also help Christian leaders throughout the world to become more effective in their ministry and assist local churches in many lands with their work.

If you would like more information about the work of World Vision, please contact one of the offices listed below:

World Vision of Britain
Dychurch House
8 Abington Street
Northampton
NN1 2AJ, United Kingdom
Tel: 0604 22964

World Vision of Australia
Box 399–C, G P O
Melbourne, 3001 Victoria
Australia
Tel: 3 699 8522

World Vision Deutschland
Postfach 1848
Adenauerallee 32
D–6370 Oberursel
West Germany
Tel: 6171 56074/5/6/7

World Vision International
Christliches Hilfswerk
Mariahilferstr 10/10
A-1070 Wien
Austria
Tel: 222–961 333/366

World Vision International
Christliches Hilfswerk
Badenserstr 87
CH-8004 Zürich
Switzerland
Tel: 1–241 7222

World Vision of Ireland
17 Percy Place
Dublin 4
Eire
Tel: 01 606 058

World Vision Singapore
Maxwell Rd
PO Box 2878
Singapore 9048
Tel: 224–8037/7419

Suomen World Vision
Kalevankatu 14 C 13
00100 Helsinki 10
Finland
Tel: 90 603422

World Vision of New Zealand
PO Box 1923
Auckland
New Zealand
Tel: 9 770 879

Stichting World
Vision Nederland
Postbus 818
3800 AV Amersfoort
The Netherlands
Tel: 33 10041

World Vision Canada
6630 Turner Valley Rd
Mississauga, Ontario
Canada L5N 2S4
Tel: 416 821 3030

World Vision United States
919 West Huntington Drive
Monrovia
CA 91016
USA
Tel: 818 303 8811

World Vision of Hong Kong
PO Box 98580
Tsim Sha Tsui Post Office
Kowloon
Hong Kong
Tel: 3–7221634